Chapter 5 Safety

They've Gotta Know
You Have Their Backs....................................146

Yes, the book does start here!

That first day of school after spring break always takes some adjustment. In Ohio, April is beautiful. Everything comes alive. The students' eyes turn toward the windows and minds toward thoughts of getting away from the classroom. It can be tough to compete with nature's call.

This April 2nd, the first day back, I decided to take on Mother Nature with an illustrated story about my vacation. My birthday invariably falls every year during spring break. It's hard to figure out what to get a suburban, middle-aged white guy for his birthday. But this year, my wife and offspring elevated their game. They bought me inversion boots. Okay, let me explain. Inversion boots allow you to hang upside down from a chin-up bar. And why, you may ask, would one want to do such a thing? Here's why:

- *It's intense lower back therapy.*
- *I get a killer ab workout.*
- *All your body fluids reverse, I'm told. (This has supposed benefits.)*
- *It's novel.*
- *I like doing bizarre workouts.*

I opened my gift, and after thank you's and laughter, I instantly knew what would monopolize the first ten minutes of class after spring break—the "Jimversion PowerPoint."

Why this story to open a book on connection?

1. Most readers skip the foreword. I hoped that a story and the upside-down-bald-guy picture might pique your interest enough to get you to read this important part of the book.
2. It introduces you, the reader, to me, the author. You get a bit of a feel for my personality.
3. I tell stories. I'm hoping you'll get used to it right away at the beginning of the book.
4. This story *is about connection*. My first thought about this crazy birthday gift (after thanking and hugging my generous family members) was to share something with my students. I took pictures of myself getting into the boots, climbing a rope to the bar, and hanging upside down. During the what-I-did-over-vacation part of class, I shared my gift. Students loved it. They saw me as human (although rather nutty); we had a good laugh; we felt connected.

My First Principle

These days, teachers have all kinds of programs, systems, standards, learning targets, and assessments to digest, integrate, implement, and embrace. It's hard to keep it all straight! Ten years ago, differentiated instruction was all the rage. Before that, educators fought pitched battles over the merits of block scheduling and all-year calendars. Even before that, the open classroom was going to solve all problems. Whether the current crop of innovations has staying power is anyone's guess.

One thing has not changed: no new program, curriculum, set of guidelines, or list of acro-

You've Gotta Connect

nyms stands a chance unless there is a strong bond between the students and their teachers. From my experience and perspective, the first principle of education is:

Teachers must learn how to connect with their students.

Why Listen to Me?

I actually teach in a high school classroom and have done so for the past twenty-eight years. I'm not a professor; I'm not an administrator; I'm not a consultant. I deal with real, live students every day, year after year. I am on the front line with you, brother and sister educators! I see the truth of the above principle work itself out every day in dozens of ways—academic, social, personal, and emotional. Students do better when they have adults in their lives who know how to connect.

Over my career, I have been to a whole slew of conferences and in-services. Some were really good; many felt like a waste of my precious time. I *do* appreciate it when the presenter teaches a specific set of skills ("here is the way to use your SmartBoard") or *is* a teacher *in the field* sharing how he or she has succeeded in a particular endeavor. This book is written in that spirit. I want to share some specific techniques and attitudes that I currently use in a real classroom.

Although plenty of my evolution came through self-discovery, I credit most of my growth to living with students and observing successful colleagues—adapting their methods to my situation and personality. This combination is the primary dynamic of this book—watch and learn from others, then adapt that to your world.

What's in This Book (and how to use it)

I am a person of action. This book is about taking action. While the style is conversational and reflective, there are many concrete directives in each chapter. These activities can be tackled individually, or they can be tackled in a communal effort. If you work through the book with colleagues or classmates, you'll build other beneficial relationships. Regardless of your arrangement, mastering the action steps is the golden ticket to transforming your relationships with students.

Each chapter addresses a theme.

Chapter 1	Commitment to the belief in connection
Chapter 2	Acceptance of all students all the time
Chapter 3	Showing students acceptance by what you say
Chapter 4	Showing students acceptance through your body language
Chapter 5	Creating a safe learning environment for students
Chapter 6	Enjoying each other in the classroom
Chapter 7	Connecting with kids in times of trouble

Each chapter follows the same structure.

Opening Anecdote: The chapter begins with a story that illustrates the importance of the topic or sets the stage for the theme.

The Pitch: This is the travel brochure. Its job is to entice you to delve into the chapter; identify the chapter's destination, significance, and relevance; and give you a preview of what will happen on the journey through this topic.

Learning Targets: The Pitch ends with a list of targets for what you will learn and be able to do.

Author Reflections: Periodically, I reflect on a past experience and tell a story to elaborate points in the chapter.

Rhetorical Questions and Student Comments: These punctuate the text in sidebars. Each is intended to provoke inquiries, challenge, and inspire. If you are working with others, these questions can provoke awesome group discussions.

Get-Connected Action Steps: Each chapter contains several action steps. These activities get you *doing* the skills that help you grow as a connector. This is where you take the ideas and apply them to your situation. You'll probably find many of these exercises enjoyable, but they take you out of your comfort zone.

Learning Targets Checklist: Each chapter ends with this summary and followup to the learning goals. Hopefully, you'll be able to check off each one for each chapter.

Humor: Finally, whenever I craft a lesson, a primary goal is to make it enjoyable for my students. As I worked on this book, I wanted to create a fun read. We have all endured tedious educational texts. I want this not to be one of them. I hope you find merriment in this book and enjoy the process of your growth.

This Could Be Your Future

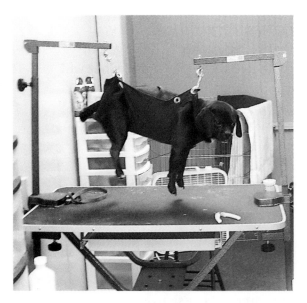

This story is mine, but it could be yours. Maybe it already is:

It's Friday morning and the alarm rings at 6:00 a.m. I arise with excitement. I'm looking forward to school today. After a good breakfast, I pack up to go. One of the things I'm packing is a jump-drive with some hilarious photos. (The wife of our school custodian recently opened a dog-grooming salon. Yesterday I took my little mutt, Dug (half-pug and half-dachshund), in for a toenail trim. The entire visit was a hoot. I took photos of the whole adventure—the dog's car ride, the salon, the custodian's wife, the other dogs in the shop, and finally my dog suspended in mid-air like a '57 Chevy waiting for his trim. I knew without a doubt that my students would love hearing about this venture.)

I get to school in plenty of time before the day starts. I got everything ready before I left yesterday, so I feel no need to rush around. I'm expecting five students to come in for my morning stretching class. I'm surprised and pleased when a shy girl from my Economics class appears with the five regulars. I can tell she is apprehensive. Once we all sprawl on the floor and stretch away stiffness, the conversation gravitates to weekend plans. Although the shy girl does not say much, she is clearly beginning to relax and enjoy herself. The fact that she showed up lets me know she is open to more connection. I'll capitalize on this opening.

Before the day begins, I have a brief pre-school morning duty monitoring the atrium where students congregate before school They are in rare form today. They're young—and it's Friday! Some are excited about the big football game tonight; others may anticipate a first date; still others are just relieved to get away from school for two days. Whatever the reasons, there is a certain energy that isn't present on Monday morning.

One of my more anxious (and way younger) colleagues surveys the mob and comments, "The natives are restless. I'm sure they are not going to be worth a damn in class today!" I don't dignify the remark with a response. Instead, I change to an uncontroversial subject while silently wondering, "Was I ever that young, or did I turn fifty right after puberty?"

My day is great. Students love the chronicle of the dog-grooming visit. They also enjoy the learning activities of the day. After the *dog story and some in-depth instruction on creating PowerPoint presentations for their big history project, I accompany them to the computer lab. While the class works in the lab, I walk around and connect with individuals. Casually, I ask questions about their work and their weekend plans. I let them know I am interested in them personally.*

The day flies by, and I am delighted when eighth period arrives. Many would shudder at the thought of a last period study hall, especially on Friday—but not I! With clear expectations set at the beginning of the semester, the study hall is a calm, relaxed setting. This is another great chance to connect warmly with students—many of whom are not in my regular classes.

After the bell rings, I look around the room and smile. I've had so many enjoyable interactions with kids today. I am terribly lucky to be a teacher.

Sure, there are plenty of disruptions and issues in my week. Some days are not as smooth as today. I make no claims that my life is perfect. I have my share of professional struggles. I have experienced serious challenges in my personal life. But a majority of my days are similar to this particular Friday. I do feel blessed for having stumbled across students, colleagues, and situations that pushed me into this world of building better connections. I've improved dramatically. So can you. If you struggle at connecting, you can learn to succeed. If you are good at connecting, you will become great!

Chapter 1

Commitment

Don't Start Class Without It

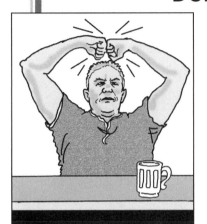

My student teacher, Charley, was nervous. He had been teaching for about three weeks and it was judgment day. His professor was coming to observe him for an entire period. He was anxious. I wasn't. I knew that he was going to shine.

I had schooled Charley well on my motto, "You've gotta connect!" A former social-studies-teacher-turned-athletic-director had thoroughly indoctrinated me on the same mantra many moons prior to this. Steve G. was an exceptionally popular teacher, and I replaced him when he moved to administration. He was a good-looking dude with a great personality (and still is). One night after a football game, Steve and I, along with a group of male administrators, went to a local watering hole. After a few adult beverages, he got off his stool, looked me dead in the eye, and said, "Jimmy, to make it in this business, you've gotta connect, Baby!"

He sounded like the sports announcer Dick Vitale. (Dick Vitale is a legendary basketball announcer at ESPN. He constantly calls people "Baby" in his thick New Jersey accent.) Steve emphasized his directive by punching his big fists together over his head to demonstrate connectivity. His pronouncement got a huge laugh from the posse that was gathered. Instinctively, I knew he was right. And his boisterous way of expressing his idea left a vivid, lasting memory.

When Charley (the aforementioned student teacher) first arrived, I let him know that my primary mission was to help him build strong relationships with the students.

"Your exciting lesson plans will have little impact if you don't bond with these kids," I told him straight out. While I didn't pound my fists together or slide into a New Jersey accent, I think Charley got the point.

Over the next few weeks, I gave Charley many specific directives. Only a few were academic in nature; the rest were detailed suggestions about how to build stronger relationships. He was an awesome pupil. His teaching content needed a little work, but I wasn't concerned because his "bedside manner" was solid.

My young protégé made a spectacular impression on his professor. He was a little apprehensive that first time she observed him, but she was wowed by his performance and was certain that he was going to be a star! Over the next few weeks she observed Charley many times, and he really settled down and excelled.

After one visit, the professor pulled me aside and asked, "Do you have ANY discipline problems?"

I shrugged my shoulders and said, "Not many."

She added, "I have been in a lot of classes, and by comparison, the atmosphere in here is fabulous. The students are lively, but they seem so relaxed and happy."

I was unprepared for her next question: "How did you create this?"

I sputtered some unsatisfactory response.

The question plagued me. How do I create this atmosphere? How much of my rapport is due to my personality and how much is based on technique?

After much thought, I came to some conclusions. It's not easy to quantify what proportion is nature and what proportion is nurture. I decided, however, **that a significant portion of my ability to connect is what I do, not who I am.** I arrived at this conclusion because

Ask Yourself:

Do I WANT to sharpen my ability to connect?

- Throughout my career I have become so much better at connecting.

- I see that connection has not been automatic; I've had to work at it.

- I can recall students with whom I did not connect or didn't have many clues as to how to connect—at least not in a way I'd be proud to repeat.

- I can recount specific times when I tried a new technique and gauged its effectiveness.

- I have had the pleasure of mentoring two student teachers that were very different in personality. I gave them the same directives, and both thrived.

- I can name colleagues that connect well with students. They have very different personal characteristics. None of them are anything like me.

Out of these ponderings and conclusions, I decided to share my techniques. And the idea for this book was born.

The Pitch

The first step in connecting to students is to make a commitment to connection! This must be a commitment to work hard and make progress at connecting with **all students** (yes, even the ones with annoying attitudes or sagging pants). Before you can pursue that goal and learn how to do it well, you've gotta get what it is! Beyond that, you need to see **why** it is absolutely critical for your students. Chapter 1 is about cementing these understandings and getting motivated to be a better connector.

Many people step into the field of education with this bold assumption: "I am popular. I make friends easily. I am very outgoing. I have lots of empathy. Getting along with kids will come naturally." However, being Mr. or Ms. Congeniality with your peers and college instructors does not necessarily translate into forging strong bonds with students once you are the teacher. Many beginning teachers quickly learn that connecting with young people is a lot harder than they anticipated. At least it's harder to connect with the reserved, reluctant, disinterested, defiant, or smart-alec students.

> ### Listen to Students
>
> *A student who feels noticed by the teacher will learn best.*

In some respects, connectivity is easily visible and clearly defined. But in other ways, it is subtle and nuanced. To become better at connecting with your students, you'll need to deepen your understanding of connection and how it works. For this chapter on **commitment**, your learning targets are:

Learning Targets

1. Show understanding of what connecting is and what it is not.

2. Show understanding of the importance of connecting.

3. Examine and advance your commitment to connecting with students.

4. Identify your current connecting skills.

5. Take steps to begin strengthening relationships with students.

As with all chapters, the ACTION STEPS of Chapter 1 will be at the heart of your journey to better connection with your students. These give you a chance to practice and grow. Follow them all! (See pages 27 to 32.)

Why Connect?

Given the choice, you would probably elect to spend time with people you like. (Most of us do!) Conversation with them is effortless. You share common interests, and there is mutual caring and respect. If the relationship is strong, you hold each other accountable. In other words, you **connect**. If you have many such relationships, you are blessed.

Now consider this scenario: You have been invited to a party. You don't want to go because you don't care for the host. However, not going would cost you socially and professionally, and you already returned the RSVP. You are stuck! You put on some nice clothes, arrive as late as possible, and endure the occasion. You keep pulling out your cell phone to check the time and hope for an urgent message that you are needed elsewhere. You don't connect with the host or his guests. You are there out of a sense of obligation. The moment finally arrives when you can tactfully leave, and you do so.

Ask Yourself:

It's likely you've had experiences in which you were forced into the midst of a group of people (or into a situation with only one or a few people) with whom you didn't jive—or worse, didn't even like. Imagine being required to spend most of every day in such a setting.

Do any of my students feel disconnected daily?

Unfortunately, **this uncomfortable (often unbearable) situation is a reality for many students. The situation is called "school."**

I hated one class in high school. I didn't care for the teacher and the feeling was mutual. Looking back, I see that I am largely to blame for the lack of rapport, but the instructor was the adult and did little to help the situation. I got such a negative vibe from this guy that eventually I thought, "the heck with it," and became a bigger pain. On the other hand, I had classes I couldn't wait to attend. The teacher was **always** the difference between these two kinds of classes. We bonded. I felt liked, welcomed, noticed. It wasn't the subject, **it was just him or it was just her!** Mastering the action steps in this book can turn you into an It's just him! or It's just her! teacher.

This is not quite what I meant by "Kids need connection."

Humans need connection. All kinds of physical, intellectual, emotional, and social situations or aspects of life just work better when you have reliable, healthy, caring, and satisfying connections. In the classroom, the reasons for and benefits of connection are legion. The brain (and the person it inhabits) needs safety in order to learn, deepen understandings, and retain ideas. A positive, comfortable, and secure relationship with the teacher is at the heart of a safe classroom. When kids connect with their teachers and feel their teachers really want to connect with them . . .

- they are happier and more productive

- they come to class and like to be there

- they are more engaged in learning activities

- their creativity is unleashed

- they learn and retain more

- they have fewer behavior issues

- they are less likely to drop out

- they feel better about themselves

- they get along better with each other

- they're more likely to be comfortable with themselves as students

- they achieve at higher levels

The positive consequences of connection multiply throughout the classroom, impacting all aspects of classroom life. An exciting and growing body of research addresses such benefits of trusting teacher-student relationships—and supports what many teachers (including this one) know from experience to be true. For more reading on this, see the list of resources on page 273.

Don't think for a minute that the benefits of connection are all for the students. Earlier I said you were blessed if you have connective relationships in your life. It may seem like a weird idea to some teachers, but your students can be blessings. You, too, will be more excited about coming to class. There are so many joys and satisfactions that accompany successful student-teacher relationships. You'll experience less stress, fewer struggles with students, and greater joy in your profession.

What Is Connection?

Some people get the wrong idea when they hear that you want to connect with students. These other people might even be teachers. (Yes, you read that right!) They may think you are needy and are just trying to be a buddy. This is an unfortunate misconception. You can care deeply for someone and have high expectations. You can bond with young people and still remain an adult. Just because you have wonderful deep relationships with your students does not mean that they walk all over you. Nor does it mean that you don't hold them accountable for their work and behavior. In fact, if you really care about a student, you will definitely set high expectations and do all you can to help him or her meet them.

Here's what effective connection looks like in a classroom:

Effective Connection Is:

1. being available
2. caring (and showing it)
3. treating students with respect
4. being a trustworthy confidant
5. showing belief in students
6. acting warm and welcoming
7. showing compassion
8. being on the student's side
9. exuding love for teaching
10. showing true interest in students
11. being a great listener
12. accepting every student

Effective Connection Is Not

1. acting like a peer
2. trying too hard to be liked
3. gossiping about students
4. having vague boundaries
5. having vague expectations
6. being unable to say "no"
7. using sarcasm
8. pampering students
9. failing to follow through
10. being phony
11. demanding respect
12. pretending to care

Turn these two lists into a poster. Copy this page and post it on your bathroom mirror, refrigerator, desk, or classroom wall. Transfer it to your computer desktop or notepad on your smart phone or other mobile device.

Get-Connected Action Steps 1.1 and 1.2, found at the end of this chapter, will plunge you right into examining your current connection and disconnection habits. **Get-Connected Action Step 1.5** will help you identify the things you already to connect well with students.

Major in Chemistry
(even if you were lost in science class)

Chemistry is the subtle side of connecting. It is difficult to define, but you certainly know it happens. There is a burgeoning online industry devoted to helping lonely people find chemistry in the dating world. The goal is building a relationship online first—bonding in terms of personality and interests. If this half of the chemistry equation clicks, then you can venture into the nerve racking face-to-face meeting realm.

Chemistry is not limited to romantic relationships. You've undoubtedly experienced its drawing power with lots of people. You may have enjoyed relationship chemistry with your parents, siblings, friends, certain coaches or teachers, a particular boss, a neighbor, and others. One thing however is certain: Attraction is laden with complex variables. What attracts one can repel another.

You won't automatically experience a spark with all students (not a positive, promising, or delightful spark anyway). (There might be sparks—but not the kind you wish.) With some, a pleasant chemistry will be natural. With others, work is required.

Fortunately, as the teacher, you are not bound to spend your life with each student the way you intend to spend your life with a perspective mate. However, you DO have to live with each student for a while. And if you don't develop some positive sparks with a student, he or she (and you) may have a miserable year. Worse, the student will not have a successful experience in your classroom. So you are behooved to expand your chemistry skills.

That guy I met last night—he's wacky. He's bald. But strangely, I'm attracted.

It is easiest to generate those warm sparks when you are open and enthusiastic about getting to know a student personally—showing interest in her interests, hobbies, strengths, opinions, and abilities. Sparks will fly when a student feels that you want him to succeed, or when you care enough to help her develop her talents. This doesn't mean there will never be any negative charges flying around with this student. But a good positive relationship—based on the student's confidence that you DO "see," believe in, and care about him or her—gives a safe and productive environment in which to handle the sizzling sparks.

Relationships are curious things. Students stride into class the first day with a host of diverse expectations. Some (unfortunately) are determined not to like you and won't give you much of a chance. Don't panic! Recognizing negative expectations and other relationship variables is an important first step in the connection process.

Twenty-five hundred years ago, the Greek philosopher Heraclites made a comment that every teacher should remember: "You cannot step twice into the same stream." So here's another chemistry lesson to apply to relationships: Change is constant. This applies to relationships as well as to the physical world. Consider these examples:

- the aloof teenager that used to be a snuggly 7-year old

- a long-time rival you now consider an ally

- the once-proud elderly parent who is now totally dependent on you

- a renewed relationship inspired by a shared loss

- a marriage strained by stress

- a marvelous catch-up moment with an old friend at a class reunion

You can forge bonds with students who are initially reluctant to be engaged. On the flip side, you can fall out of favor with those with whom you felt an incredible connection. There is great potential in this simple awareness. Embrace the fluid nature of your relationships with students.

You step into a new stream dozens of times each day with your students. Never assume that the stream will be the same as it was yesterday.

Part of the science of chemistry lies in knowing that you have to repeat a process again and again with the right ingredients to get the right results. Mix in a judgmental attitude, a drop of neglect, a sarcastic retort, or a few manipulative moves—or forget to stir with the right amount of care, or mistakenly shake something up with a pinch of threat or humiliation—and the whole thing will go awry. You can damage a good relationship. But you can also change the ingredients and tactics and rescue a struggling connection or create a new one that seemed impossible. So brush up on chemistry well enough to forge, monitor, and nurture bonds with students diligently—and daily.

Try **Get-Connected Action Steps 1.3 and 1.4, found** at the end of this chapter, for some reflection on your chemistry with students.

Ask Yourself:

Have I ever set back a relationship with a moment of neglect or a wrong word?

Author's Reflection

In my first week of college, a guy on my floor in the dorm made repeated friendship overtures. He had gone to a rival high school, and we had competed against each other in track meets. He used to beat one of my best friends in the half mile; these close calls infuriated my friend. It didn't help that this kid paraded around at meets putting on a big show. As far as I was concerned, he was still an obnoxious enemy.

When my parents asked if I had made new friends yet, I described the situation. Dad told me to cut my assertive pursuer some slack.

I remember him saying, "I am sure he is just lonely. Give him a break! You never know—you may end up with a new friend."

The next day, I heard the familiar knock. He challenged me to play an electronic football game. I took my father's suggestion, accepted the dare, and the next two hours just evaporated. It turned out that this guy was pretty darned funny. When I would win a game, he would have a conniption. He would swear and make violent gestures. When I would lose, he would give me the business! There was no doubt about it: I was having a blast. The flamboyance that used to make me burn with rage in high school I now found enchanting. My paradigm shifted. My father was right—I found a new friend. And, we have been friends for over 30 years. Relationships constantly mutate. (Anyone who has been married for more than five minutes totally gets this.)

My administrator buddy in the bar after the football game—the one who pounded his fists together and implored me to connect—was right. Students who connect with their teachers thrive. With a little motivation, I started to think about what connection is, why to do it, and how to do it. I watched other teachers do it well (or not do it). I began to notice how things changed as I attend to connection. I'm so jazzed about the difference this makes! So I hope you'll get motivated to embark on or continue on the electrifying path to stronger connections with students.

Listen to Students

I feel connected to a teacher who talks as comfortably with the kids as she does with other teachers.

In this chapter so far, you have seen what connection is and what it is not. You've had a bit of a chemistry lesson about the sparks and fluidity of connection. Now it is time to dig deeper and grow further in your ability to connect with your students. Follow the actions steps below. Then, don't neglect to finish the chapter by summarizing what you learned in the chapter. See the **Learning Targets Checklist** on the final page of this chapter.

Get-Connected! Action Steps

Action Step 1.1 Connection Do's and Don'ts

Apply some connection do's and don'ts to your own experience. Here, you will summarize personal examples that illustrate the importance of as many of the concepts as you can recall. Take this step alone or in a small group. If you are working with others on a team, you might divide and conquer by splitting up the items. Also, temporarily separate from each other so you have time and space to reflect on your own.

1. Use the **Connection Do's and Don'ts** forms on pages 33 to 36. Under each item, write a brief description of an event that demonstrates the directive. These experiences could be from an interaction involving you, or from one you observed. Your reflections may be from your student days, or from your professional experiences. Challenge yourself to draw positive examples from situations you have witnessed. In other words, learn from a role model. The goal is enlightenment, not self-promotion. But if there is a personal example of which you are particularly proud, by all means use it. Likewise, try to recall negative examples where you were in the center of the action. We often learn more from our mistakes than our successes.

2. If you are fortunate to be working through the book with others, reconvene and share what you wrote. Be prepared for some interesting dialogue! Then, be sure to keep the two lists, **Effective Connection Is** and **Effective Connection Is Not**, in front of your eyes all year long. (See page 22.)

Action Step 1.2 Repeat That!

Repeat Action Step 1.1 again during the school year. Compare your responses. Reflect on what you have learned. Then repeat it each year. Begin to focus on interactions with students during the current school year. Once you start employing the tactics outlined in this book, your *Do's* side of the ledger will be a masterpiece of evolutionary evidence. Your *Don'ts* side will be meager.

Action Step 1.3 It's Just Her! It's Just Him!

Let's hope that you experienced good chemistry with some teachers in your past. (It's hard to imagine anyone going into education if they didn't have inspirational role models.) Let's investigate what made one or more of those teachers the *it was just her!* (or *him!*) instructor for you.

1. Interview 20 people. If are you working in a group, each member could interview 5 people. Or, you could pair up and take turns interviewing one another. The interviewee (person answering)

will be contemplating her or his ideal teacher. Use the questions on the **The Teacher I Prefer** form on page 37 or design your own form and questions. The interviewee will be given a choice about traits they prefer in their instructors. She or he must choose the first trait or second. (Granted, some of the questions are about teaching methods, but what tactics a teacher favors reveals aspects of their personality.)

28

2. Ask the interviewee to explain a rationale for their choice.

3. Next, compile a group score. Tally the results to determine if there is any consensus on traits. (Use the **Teacher Preference Score Card** on page 38 or create your own.) Also, record some of the most interesting responses. You may see big differences or slight differences in the preferences. Keep in mind that this is a small sample. Even when there is consensus, a preference may be inspired by diverse rationales. Two individuals may desire a female teacher, but they may choose so for entirely different reasons. So listen and record the explanations or comments that underlie the choices.

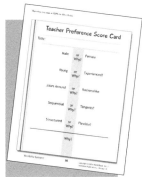

4. If you are working on this action step with others, discuss your findings. Share your observations with the group. However, it is more important to listen intently to your colleagues. You'll learn more in receiving mode than in broadcasting mode. This action step and ensuing discussion will expose further evidence of the diversity of student expectations when it comes to instructors.

Students come to class with many diverse preferences and expectations. You have no control over this. Building relationships is the goal, and you must recognize that some arrive in class predisposed not to cooperate. Embrace that you face many hurdles and variables and then strive to win over reluctant students. This is achievable because connectivity is fluid. It can be gained and unfortunately, it can be lost!

You've Gotta Connect

Action Step 1.4 Up for Grabs

Do the following exercise in a reflection mode. (Respond to the prompts in a journal or mentally.) Or, do this with a colleague or friend or in a small group.

Think of a past relationship wherein your initial response was not to like the person but later grew quite fond of him or her (a teacher, coach, blind date, boss, neighbor, classmate, co-worker, or the person who eventually became a partner or spouse). Respond to the following prompts:

1. Tell who the person was and why you were in a position to have a relationship.

2. Explain what initially repelled you about the person.

3. Describe the event that changed the dynamic.

4. How did this new relationship enrich your life?

Now flip your perspective. Recall a relationship that seemed solid— but took a dive. You were the best of buddies, the teacher's pet, your boss' favorite, the coach's right hand man or woman, best friends on the job, or romantic partners. This activity can be sad, but it is important. Respond to the following prompts:

1. Describe your relationship prior to the deterioration.

2. What attracted you to this person?

3. What caused the alienation?

4. How were you affected by the loss of this relationship?

Any relationship can be up for grabs at any time. Connectivity can be gained, and it can be lost. You have a chance to win over a student who comes to class predisposed to like you. You can get to know a seemingly annoying or unlikable student and find the lovable within. When relationships seem broken, there is usually an opportunity for repair and reconciliation—if you watch for it and take the risk to fix it. Conversely, just because you have a strong relationship with a student, you should NEVER take that bond for granted.

Action Step 1.5 What's Working? Start There!

Whether you have thought about it or not, you probably already have some great ways that you connect with students. (Hmm, if not—are you sure you're in the right profession?) This action step will focus and build on what you are already doing right.

1. Review the lists found on page 22 in this chapter, **Effective Connection Is** and **Effective Connection Is Not**.

2. Find a list of all your students' names. Think about each student. Did you have a connection with him or her that you believe helped him or her with one of these areas in the past week? Circle or note names of students. (It will be hard not to notice names you can't circle! That's useful, too.)
   Because of some connective action, the student . . .

   • is happier and/or more productive

   • comes to class and likes to be there

   • knows that you are interested in him or her

- shows more engagement in learning activities

- had his or her creativity unleashed

- noticeably learns or retains more

- has fewer behavior issues

- feels better about herself or himself

- gets along better with other students

- appears to be comfortable with herself or himself as a student

- achieves at higher levels

3. Make a copy of **My Connecting Talents** on page 39. Complete this thoughtfully. Choose some of the student names you circled and describe three of the specific connective actions you took.

4. Keep your mind and eyes open to the tactics, words, gestures, attitudes, and actions you already use that offer good connection to students. Keep jotting these down.

5. Make a commitment to purposefully use a talent from your list in each class every day for the next week.

Connection Do's

Do

1. be available

_____

_____

2. care (for real!)

_____

_____

3. treat students with respect

_____

_____

4. be a trustworthy confidant

_____

_____

5. show belief in students

_____

_____

6. be warm and welcoming

_____

_____

You've Gotta Connect

Connection Do's (cont.)

Do

7. show compassion

_____

_____

8. be on the student's side

_____

_____

9. exude love for teaching

_____

_____

10. show true interest in students

_____

_____

11. be a great listener

_____

_____

12. demonstrate acceptance

_____

_____

Connection Don'ts

Don't

1. act like a peer

_____

_____

2. try too hard to be liked

_____

_____

3. gossip about students

_____

_____

4. fail to set boundaries

_____

_____

5. fail to set high expectations

_____

_____

6. be unable to say no

_____

_____

You've Gotta Connect

Don't

Connection Don'ts (cont.)

7. be sarcastic

_____

_____

8. pamper students

_____

_____

9. fail to follow through

_____

_____

10. pretend to care

_____

_____

Analyze your lists as you respond to the following prompts:

Which list was easier to complete (Do's or Don'ts)?

What emotions surfaced when responding to the prompts from the Do's list?

Did the recollections from the Don'ts list make you uncomfortable? If so, why?

If you are fortunate to be working through this activity with others, reconvene and share what you wrote. Be prepared for some interesting dialogue!

The Teacher I Prefer...

Circle one of the two traits within each question.

Would you rather have a male or female teacher?

Why?

Do you prefer younger or more experienced teachers?

Why?

Do you like your teachers to dress casually or professionally?

Why?

Do you like a teacher who jokes around or is business-like?

Why?

Do you prefer a teacher who presents things in strict sequence or one who goes off on tangents?

Why?

Do you like a teacher who is flexible or more structured?

Why?

What is another trait you prefer in a teacher?

Why?

Teacher Preference Score Card

Tally:

Male	or Why?	Female
Young	or Why?	Experienced?
Jokes Around	or Why?	Businesslike
Sequential	or Why?	Tangents?
Structured	or Why?	Flexible?
	Why?	

My Connecting Talents

My most successful connecting talent or technique is

_____

_____

I had satisfying, effective connections with these
students in the past week.

1. _____   2. _____

3. _____   4. _____

Here's a description of three situations in which I connected well with a
student or group of students in the past week. (Tell what you did.)

1	2

3

You've Gotta Connect

✓ Learning Targets Checklist

To summarize what you have learned in this chapter,
check ✓ if you . . .

_____ can describe how teachers who connect have impact.

_____ can identify some characteristics of what connecting is and what
it is not.

_____ can describe how really knowing a student affects the chemistry
between you and her or him.

_____ are ready to take steps toward becoming an *it's just her* or *it's
just him* teacher.

_____ have ideas about how to win over reluctant students.

_____ understand how you can damage a relationshipwith a student
with whom you have a strong bond.

_____ have identified your already-existing connecting behaviors or
strategies.

_____ can verify that you have completed most of the Get-Connected
Action Steps in this chapter.

Chapter 2   Acceptance

It's Not the Kids; It's YOU

It's Friday night, and you've invited some friends along to the football game at the high school where you teach. Your students are out in force. They are only marginally interested in what's taking place on the field. Mostly, they are consumed with socializing. The boys are doing all kinds of posturing, and the girls are dressed to attract the boys' attention. The majority of the students is not even in the stands, but milling about—flirting, gossiping, huddling, watching.

Your friends are unnerved by this rabble. Many of the youngsters are dressed or act like *geeks, skaters, gangstahs, hipsters, emos, mean girls,* or some other cultural tangent.* Your companions have been considering having a child, and this whole scene gives them pause. The young wife is getting intimidated; the young husband's adrenaline is starting to percolate.

The kids acknowledge you in loud, aggressive voices, "HEY, MR. OR MS. SO AND SO!" They barely notice your anxious friends; their focus is on you—but only briefly, and then it's back on each other.

---

* Geeks—socially inept persons, often brainy
  Skaters—kids who ride skateboards or dress like punks
  Gangstas—wannabe thugs
  Jocks—super-conceited dudes
  Hipsters—independent, counterculture kids (often wear thrift store attire)
  Emos—punk music addicts, known for greasy black hair, wool hats, and scarves
  Mean Girls—aggressive bullies who use exclusion, nasty talk, and rumors to intimidate and manipulate other girls

The wife remarks, "How do you face these kids every day?"

Have you been part of such a scenario? Questions about how you can survive with "those kids" might be familiar, particularly if you teach middle school or high school students. You might answer the question with great pride. After all, you are doing a job that a lot of adults find intimidating or maddening to the point where they may become violent. Unlike your anxious friends, you are as cool as the other side of the pillow in such a setting. These are **your** kids—your peeps! You know what they are trying to do; you see it all the time. You're rather charmed by it.

Or maybe not. Maybe you feel embarrassed and uncomfortable. You might be sorry you brought your friends to the setting. You might mumble some answer, such as "Oh, I grin and bear it" or "This gets worse every year. Fortunately, I can retire soon."

Plenty of adults, including teachers, hold the younger generation (especially when gathered in "packs") in low or close-to-low regard. Guess what? Many adults, for many generations, have held the younger generations in low regard. You can choose to continue the pattern, or you can look through the behaviors and attires and accept the person.

The Pitch

You connect with students by accepting them. So many problems with students originate from the teacher—the teacher's attitudes, biases, fears, insecurities, judgments, habits, or past personal experiences with school. The teacher's own "stuff" gets in the way of acceptance. Even worse, sometimes the teacher's attitudes and actions actually cause disconnection. As a teacher, it can keep you from the kinds of healthy relationships with students that nurture them, give them the best chance at success, and offer genuine satisfaction for you. This is more likely to happen if you are unaware of your disconnecting personal attitudes and habits.

In this chapter, I'll push you to pay close attention to your behaviors that show acceptance or nonacceptance toward students and to the feelings or attitudes that lie behind these behaviors. Accepting students is not always easy. You want so badly for your students to evolve into kind, responsible, productive, and ultimately happy adults. Yet your desires for them are often frustrated. They make ridiculous choices; they don't apply themselves; and sometimes they can be downright cruel. You can become so exasperated that you feel like giving up. Don't quit! You can change some things. There is one thing you can control (probably the only thing). That is yourself—your viewpoints, your attitudes, and your behavior.

You have the best shot at effecting positive change in your students if you change YOU. To do this, you'll need to honestly examine your biases and behaviors around acceptance, attend to environments or nostalgia that feed nonacceptance of students, and take steps toward accepting all your students fully. It may not be easy; but I guarantee that you will find renewed energy, joy, and connection with your students. And this will positively affect so many of the processes, details, and successes in your classroom.

For this chapter on **acceptance**, your learning targets are:

Learning Targets

1. Examine your attitudes about this generation of students in general and about individual students in particular.

2. Identify nostalgic ideas that keep you from accepting students.

3. Notice places and people that negatively influence your attitudes towards students.

4. Learn how your biases affect your behavior toward students.

5. Take steps to start getting beyond your biases.

Take a Close Look
(Your biases are showing)

"But I'm a teacher!" you protest. "I care about students. I accept them. They know they can trust me!" Yah, that's what I thought, too. I went into teaching because I liked being around young people—had a knack for being with them. I'm not saying that this is not true of you or me. I will say that when I started paying close attention, I noticed all kinds of little (and big) signs that brought my acceptance of the kids into question. I'll ask you to look at some of the areas that leapt out (or crept out) when I got an "up-close" view of myself and my colleagues.

1. How do you feel about students' characteristics, behaviors, habits, interests such as these?

   • treatment of each other

   • manners

   • language

   • attitudes toward punctuality

   • attention to homework

   • view of themselves as students

   • attire

   • hairstyles

   • body adornment

   • language

   • regard for school property

   • use of social media

   • gestures

   • body gestures, contortions, habits, odors

   • hygiene

   • ways of communicating with each other

- ways they treat each other
- fears, protective behaviors
- attitudes toward adults
- music
- behavior choices
- study choices
- choices of friends
- subcultures
- parents or families
- past school behavior
- after-school interests

2. How do these feelings get translated or projected to your students (consciously or unconsciously on your part)?

3. How often do you act or react with annoyance, impatience, disregard, or disgust toward one of your students because of behavior, attitude, or choices?

4. How often do you show approval of a certain student in a way that clearly suggests disapproval toward other students?

5. Which of your behaviors could your students interpret as showing favoritism?

6. How easily could your students identify your favorite (and least favorite) students in the class?

Yep, you get the idea! If you start to dig and if you try to be honest, you'll have some revealing answers to these questions. If you are stymied, ask some students for help. You can be sure they are able to see your biases. We all must identify and admit to these. The first step toward accepting our students is recognizing where we don't—even when we thought we did. Some of the action steps later in this chapter will help focus on doing this.

Get an Attitude Adjustment

Many adults hear the word *acceptance* (in relationship to students) and immediately "go confrontational." To them, *acceptance* equals *endorsement*. It's not. If someone cannot disentangle *acceptance* from *endorsement*, I wonder if she or he might better choose to fix washing machines or design rocket ships instead of teach.

So what **is** *acceptance*? To me, it is having a firm grasp of the situation, getting out of any state of denial, dealing with reality. See what IS and get used to it. (I did not say approve of it.)

Once you identify your own biases and pay attention to your own attitudes, you can

- start looking at your students realistically
- get away from whatever fears, past experiences, and stereotypes crowd your judgment
- look—really look—at every student
- look beyond the behavior or appearance to see the person
- do your best to get a feel for what it is to be in your students' shoes
- learn about their viewpoints, their priorities
- pay attention to their interests
- see their gifts; look for what delights you about each one
- find out what drives them, what inspires them, what scares them

When students step into your presence, they come laden with characteristics and behaviors that immediately please, worry, annoy, or frustrate you. You can influence many things in your students' lives. But face it, there are a whole lot of things that you cannot change. You can fight students, threaten them, struggle against them, give out citations, or have epic conniptions. But you can't change the kids. When you reach these walls, know this wonderful fact. **There is something you can change—and that is yourself.** You can change your attitude. Yes, and you can change the way you respond to a situation, behavior, or attitude.

This may sound simple, but it is HUGE! When you can't change the kid or the situation, change YOU. This opens up a realm of possibilities and hope! It allows you to build better relationships with students. It allows you to see them in a different light. It smooths the way for you to effectively influence the things you CAN change.

You can't connect to someone you don't accept. No student who feels unaccepted by you is ever going to want to connect with you. Acceptance means embracing every student as he is or where she is. It means accepting what each group of kids brings into your presence. You can do that if you adjust any attitudes that dis, discount, or discard one or more students. **Get-Connected Action Steps 2.1, 2.3, 2.4, and 2.7** will all move you well along in the process of identifying your attitudes and biases toward students and making some adaptations.

Author's Reflection

I have often thought that being a dad is more challenging than being a teacher. Parenting, after all, is 24/7 with no vacations. For me, it has been my best learning experience and helped me become a more compassionate educator. Sometimes when I hear colleagues complain about their students' parents, I become uneasy. They may not know the whole story. A student's family may face significant burdens.

Recently, my son developed quite a fondness for tattoos. This gave me great pause. Intellectually, I knew the tattoo debate is a great example of a generation gap. I also knew there were things I valued as a teen my parents could neither understand nor stomach. However, I could not imagine what could possibly motivate him to want a tattoo; tattoos were not on my radar when I was a teen. But here he was, my pride and joy, asking for one, and there were plenty of role models sporting them at our school. But still, I argued, a tattoo is SO permanent.

As is the case with most difficult decisions, there were many variables to consider. My wife and I went through an agonizing evaluation of whether or not to permit the tattoo. By our nature, we are not controlling parents. We like to encourage our kids to be independent decision makers. (Why did we ever think that was a good idea?) This decision was a tough one!

We made a list of all of our objections. We took that commentary running through our heads and wrote it down. The act of putting it down on paper forced us to look squarely at our biases. Next, we evaluated each objection. We decided to challenge each of our "self-talk" statements, trying to consider the issue from our son's perspective.

The lists here show our work. Some objections, we discovered, were purely generational. As we did this work, we pushed ourselves to examine and try to adjust our attitudes. This was such an enlightening experience that we've used it many times since. (I'll lead you to try it too in **Get-Connected Action Step 2.2** at the end of the chapter.)

As you probably guessed, my son got his tattoo. Only time will tell whether we made the right decision. I do, however, feel comfortable with the way we came to the verdict. We analyzed the reasonableness of each of our objections. Once we saw his

Our Negative Mental Commentary about Tattoos	Challenging Our Negative Mental Commentary about Tattoos
1. They are permanent.	1. Tattoo removal will be common in the future.
2. He needs to wait until he is 18.	2. It is a memorial to a dear friend—a healing.
3. Tattoos look ridiculous or disgusting.	3. Not to this generation.
4. If he gets one, he will probably want more.	4. He will be 18 soon and can get as many as he wants anyway.
5. When he is older, he will consider this decision a mistake.	5. Maybe not, but it will be his to live with.
6. He needs to find more constructive outlets.	6. Designing tattoos means applying his artistic talents— which is very constructive.

David

tattoo, we were blown away by the beautiful creation. David expresses himself kinesthetically. He's athletic and artistic, and his art has great meaning to him. But there's more to the story. Woody Bagwell, the tattoo artist, was drawn (no pun intended) to David's work. Woody offered David an apprenticeship. Thrilled, our son took his creative inclinations (inclinations we did not understand—inclinations we found threatening) and used them for a paycheck—an elusive goal of every artist.

I hope our story will keep you from applying negative labels too hastily to the expressions of today's youth. Yes, your initial reactions may have merit, and yes, their appetites may lead to regret. But before you leap to those conclusions, objectively examine your attitudes. Some of your fears (while well-intentioned), may be irrational and bigoted. See the image created by our talented teenage son. His girlfriend died. This is his tribute to her.

You've Gotta Connect

Beware the Teachers' Lounge
(and other toxic locations)

In many high schools, the place where teachers hang out is called *the faculty lounge* or *the teachers' lounge*. Other apt names might be *the den of iniquity* or *the grievance café*. Do I need to elaborate? Okay, I won't—much.

I do ask educators to think about questions such as these: "What goes on in the faculty room that nurtures or hinders your acceptance of students?" and "What do you hear or say that threatens or deepens connections with students?"

Ask Yourself:

How do my biases show?

Start paying attention to this. Notice what kinds of comments adults make about students when students are not nearby. Notice the comments you make. Notice your own level of comfort or discomfort with the conversation. What is the attitude that floats around the room? Does it feed your tendency to gripe? Or, does it feed your healthier tendencies to advocate for students and uplift them?

Whether or not we like it (or want to admit it), our environment influences us all. Most of us as teachers are keenly aware of how social groups influence the behavior and attitudes of our students. We watch the snobbery, drama, cruelty, or power of peers in groups. We know the influences of the cliques in the lunchroom, playground, or quad. We pick up plenty about the effects of the locker room or the smoker's corner near the high school. Too often, however, we are oblivious to influences on ourselves. Let your awareness be heightened! You are not immune to your peer group either. It is hard to walk into a negative, griping atmosphere and stay positive. You're tired, you just had a tough class, and your defenses are down. It feels good (for a short while) to get some empathy. But does it really help? Does it feel good in the long run?

Your teachers' room may not be a place where students (or their parents) are dissected or criticized. Hopefully, not! But do start noticing your environment. Identify places that are toxic when it comes to accepting students. Make it a point to stay away—at least until you feel strong enough to combat the negativity with compliments, hope, and advocacy!

Kiss Nostalgia Goodbye

A few weeks ago, my students were doing an extended project in class. I thought they'd enjoy some background music. I got out my iPod and chose some of my favorite 1970's R&B tunes. I was sure they'd think this was cool and that it would lend some energy to their work. They didn't; it didn't.

"How can you **not** like this music? These are some solid jams!" I started in on adult babble trying to convince them of my wisdom and put my taste up against theirs as superior. They glazed over. The next thing out of my mouth was, "When I was in high school . . ."

As their eyes glazed over, mine opened. Oh, no! I had turned into one of those teachers who droned on and on, lost in another era. I can picture one of my junior high school teachers. He seemed like a museum exhibit. I thought he was 100. (He was probably much younger than I am now.) Just like him, I had become Mr. Out-of-Touch, sliding into my editorial mode, giving out the message that the good old days were superior. Suddenly I knew that my students were hearing, "When I was in school, BLAH, BLAH, BLAH."

And I knew they were thinking, "No one cares about your thousand-year-old music. We weren't even alive then." And I knew they were wishing they could get out their own iPods.

You've Gotta Connect

Do you long for the kind of respect that students in your era were trained to pay to teachers? Do you remember earlier teaching years when parents were more involved and students were less hostile? Do you wish you were back in that other school where you taught before—where you had fewer discipline problems and struggled with fewer slackers? Do you pine for last year when you got through all the material with students who behaved pretty well and seemed to enjoy learning? Do you dread your fifth-period class, wishing they had the self-control and self-motivation that your fourth-period class has? (Yes, teachers can even be nostalgic about something great that happened an hour ago!)

Ask Yourself:

What nostalgia keeps me distant from my students?

Ahhh . . . how comforting it is to slip into those memories! I don't know any teacher who does not have bouts of nostalgia. But hear me now: **you've gotta let go of it!** This nostalgia interferes with connection to present students. It keeps you from seeing THESE students—their needs and gifts. That young woman or man is not the eager student that you were. These students are not those other kids in those other schools or other eras. They are not even last period's class. (Sorry to discourage you, but at this brief juncture in the space-time continuum, they are not even who they were yesterday!)

Many social studies teachers (like me) love to compare the past and present. There is nothing wrong with being nostalgic on occasion. But nostalgia can stray far from objective truth; its emotional power can skew your vision; it can injure. When nostalgia takes you away from the students that you have been blessed with the power to influence, it is far from harmless. I caution all educators about nostalgia. This moment is all we ever have with each student. Nostalgia can absolutely detour efforts to accept a student for what she or is in this moment.

Author's Reflection

I've always remembered kindergarten with fondness. I can't look at the 5-year-old Jimmy without the feelings of a September Tuesday in 1966 washing over me. Full of excitement and feeling like a big boy, I headed off into a world of adventure. I loved the independence of the walk to school. I had fun at school. I was popular. The teacher liked me. I felt like part of something big and wonderful. As I look back, I have only positive memories of pleasant times in those early years of school.

I was clueless at the time, but now I see that plenty of circumstances out of my control contributed to the happiness I remember. I was a remarkably well-positioned member of a privileged class. As far as success in school, I had ALL the right boxes checked:

☑ *male*
☑ *white*
☑ *Christian*
☑ *athletic*
☑ *lived with both biological parents*
☑ *happily married parents*
☑ *heterosexual*
☑ *financially stable parents*
☑ *fairly intelligent*

But things weren't so rosy for classmates who weren't able to check all those boxes. (This included a lot of kids.) In 1966, our school system emphasized conformity. Granted, you couldn't control your genetics or your parents, but other variables were a different matter. Kids came to school well groomed. All males were required to wear slacks, not jeans. All shirts had to have a collar. The high school boys were not permitted to have facial hair nor long hair for that matter. If you were female, wearing pants was not acceptable. Most girls wore knee socks with their dresses or skirts.

You've Gotta Connect

Discipline was based on fear. Corporal punishment was the corner-stone. It was not uncommon for adult staff members to threaten male students (and an occasional outgoing female). Those threats were not always idle in nature.

Sexism was the norm. Young females who wanted to become professionals in business, medicine, law, or politics, were not given much (if any) encouragement. High school girls who got pregnant just disappeared. Schools let them know in subtle, or sometimes not so subtle, ways that they were no longer welcome. The young "baby daddy" often went on with his plans and suffered no repercussions, as far as the school was concerned.

It's easy to get sentimental about the "good" part of my innocent "good ole days" in primary school. Just look at that picture! Wow! Kids dressed up for school pictures in those days! What a dream it must have been to be a teacher then!

I've learned to mistrust such nostalgia and to temper it. In reality, I have no desire to be back in that era. I prefer celebrating diversity rather than conformity. Maybe kids combed their hair, but all that order and the clean-cut manners really does not lure me (well, not much).

I could go on a long time about whether the school experiences you remember with great affection were as great as you remember them. Nostalgia tends to include elements of sugarcoating and reinvention. So get those nostalgia sensors sharpened. See the past realistically. Even more important, become keenly aware of the moments when it disconnects you from present students. If you look at a student and wish for her to be like you were as a student, you do not accept her. When you long for this class to have the passion about your poetry unit that last year's juniors had, these kids will feel your lack of acceptance.

Please remember: You and your students are citizens of the present. True, you might long for the mother country (back when you were in high school or some other glorious past moment), but you're here now, and that's not changing. Furthermore, your students are quite content in the present. It's all they know, and teaching is all about them.

What nostalgic attachments do I need to bid farewell?

Trade Annoyance for Acceptance

Many young people get into education because they loved school and were good at it. They were student leaders and wanted to share their enthusiasm for the entire enterprise with the next crop of young people. This motivation, while certainly noble, **can** be a real hindrance to the goal of connecting with today's students. Our classrooms are full of students who don't experience much joy or success. Imagine how it feels to have to participate every single day in something about which you feel little hope for success. Imagine the insecurity and stress. Imagine how unhelpful it is to sit in front of someone who has mastered what you feel you cannot—and hear that person saying enthusiastically (or worse, in a shaming tone), "All you need to do is apply yourself."

I was not academically motivated as an adolescent. I looked at school as a huge social opportunity. I loved sports and had many friends, but I thought that most of my classes were boring and pointless. I wished that those kids in the National Honor Society and others who bragged about their GPAs would curb their neediness and stop trying to extract compliments from everyone. I was a friendly guy, so I liked many of my teachers; but I thought most of their lessons were dull. When I pictured them as teenagers, I envisioned them as annoying clones of the striving peers mentioned a few sentences ago. I also did my fair share of experimentation with partying and girls. I was your typical slacker.

It is hard for nonslackers to understand slackers. In my experience, slackers are not very receptive to long passionate lectures from nonslackers about what they need to do to straighten their lives out. Most slackers must come to the realization that their lives could be much better, in their own sweet time. That is what happened to me. Sometime late in my junior year, I came to the conclusion that I wanted more out of life and that my current trajectory was going to be unsatisfactory. I had been given "the lecture" by a number of nonslackers, but to be honest with you, it was counterproductive. Just to spite them, I did exactly what they told me not to do.

This leads me to a small piece of wisdom I think I have to share because I was one of those kids that frustrates, annoys, or worries so many teachers: I won't say that you shouldn't try to be honest with kids. You do have a responsibility to tell kids the truth about their futures and their choices. But if you connect with them, you have a much greater chance of getting through to them. And you can't connect if you don't accept.

In this chapter, I encourage you to trade annoyance for acceptance. I believe you do this by:

1. examining your soul and your behavior to see all the ways you secretly, consciously or unconsciously discriminate against, dis, disregard, distrust, disparage, or dismiss any individuals or group as a whole.

2. falling in love with your students again. Try to remember what it was like to be their age— even though your era was different. Look at the persons, not their annoying stances or dumb choices. Try to find joy and enjoyment in each one. Get to know them.

I'll add that I mean accept **all** your students. Maybe you were a slacker, like I was. So you find it easier to accept the slackers. Maybe you need to work on accepting the high achievers or teacher pleasers. Maybe the jocks or the geeks annoy you. Open your heart to them all! Students can plainly read acceptance or nonacceptance.

I had a funny biology teacher back in high school. He was a good ole boy with some classic sayings. He loved his subject and would often repeat this adage, "There are three choices for any species: migrate; mutate; or lie down and die." This line was delivered with a thick southeastern Ohio drawl. Sometimes we would drift toward the door prior to the bell ringing, and he would chime out, "Now you kids quit that migrating!" His familiar refrain about species can be applied to lots of situations in life.

I find myself applying his mantra to teaching. The first choice, migration, is a very viable option for many. According to *nea today*, the online journal of the National Education Association, migration is high in the teaching profession (not migration from school to school, but migration right out of the profession).

> *Nationally, the average turnover for all teachers is 17 percent, and in urban school districts specifically, the number jumps to 20 percent, according to the National Center for Education Statistics. The National Commission on Teaching and America's Future proffers starker numbers, estimating that one-third of all new teachers leave after three years, and 46 percent are gone within five years. Almost a third of America's teachers leave the field sometime after their first three years of teaching, and almost half leave after five years (Kopkowski 2008).*

There are multiple reasons for this high rate of attrition, and many research studies identify the reasons. All teachers can probably name colleagues that would have been better suited for other professions. I lament the loss of many teachers who might have stayed and been good for students, had the pressures, lack of respect, red tape, or compensation not been so troublesome. But as I mentor young teachers, I also beg, "If teaching is not right for you—for the sake of the students take the bold step and migrate."

Listen to Students

A teacher who accepts me will try to find out what I like about myself.

The final option given by my former biology teacher was to lie down and die. Most of us have witnessed a death of sorts among a few colleagues. They became closed down and rigid. They became negative about the students. Many of these folks are lost in nostalgia and tell anyone who will listen about the way things used to be or the ways things used to be handled. Such conversations are tiresome. These teachers suffer a professional death and become isolated and marginalized. Undoubtedly, they are not positively connected to students. If you feel yourself in or sliding into this category, I'd like to argue you back to life if I could. One way that I know to revive or reinvigorate a teaching career is to "change up" the whole way you relate to students. Try the connection steps in this book. You might experience a resurrection! Yes! Connection to students has that power.

The biology teacher's middle option was to mutate—or I could say—to grow or to evolve. This is the healthiest choice. It does not mean that you have to start sagging your pants. It means it is always healthier to accept students for who they are. That does not mean that you have to embrace everything this generation of students stands for; it certainly doesn't mean that you have no hope of influencing them. In education, I believe "mutate" means to change yourself, change your attitude, and accept the students. It's the rational option.

It was one of those bleak Ohio February days. These are the "dog days" in the school year—the dead of winter, all the freshness of the season and the school year long gone, and spring break too far away. The students and staff were getting, as my mom used to say, "a bit bucky." As I exited the building in the darkening afternoon, I held the door for a young colleague. The students were doing their usual post-school parking lot posturing ritual: revving their engines and blaring their music with staggering amounts of bass. The young woman, who was all of maybe 28, looked at me and said, "I can't believe these kids. Jim, did we act like that?"

I started to smile. "Yes, 10 years ago and 20 years ago, students were aggressive with their cars in high school parking lots!" She laughed. I laughed. We both knew that this behavior (which might for a moment seem obnoxious) is what teenagers have always done—and we did it too. Any disapproval we may have felt melted away in the waning afternoon sun.

In this chapter, there's been a lot of talk about acceptance. It's time to put it all to work in your own way. The action steps below will gently guide you along a path to examining your biases, pondering your acceptance behaviors and patterns, changing some attitudes, and taking some first steps toward changing behaviors.

Then, don't neglect to finish the chapter by summarizing what you learned in the chapter. See the **Learning Targets Checklist** on the final page of Chapter 2.

Get-Connected! Action Steps

Action Step 2.1   Attitude Inventory

It's time to examine your biases and attitudes about the behavior, attitudes, and interests of this present generation of students (in particular, the attributes you hate!) Make a list of what bugs you. Include every thing about this age group of this generation that you find abhorrent, appalling, or just annoying.

1. This list here comes from my own self-examination and conversation with teachers of adolescents and pre-adolescents. Think about your most frequently voiced (or secretly thought) irritations.

2. Use the **Attitude Inventory** form on page 69 to make your list of complaints. Borrow as many from my list as represent you, but by all means make your own list.

3. Circle all the issues or attributes on the list that you can influence—directly or indirectly. These are areas where you are reasonably confident you could help students improve (which, by the way, is a noble endeavor).

4. For each of the items you circle, identify at least one action you can take to influence your students' habits, attitudes, or actions in a way that does not show judgment, disgust, or disregard. Write this beneath the item on the **Attitude Inventory** form. Plan to put these actions into practice right away.

Everything I abhor about this generation . . .

1. their music
2. their clothes
3. their manners
4. their lack of respect
5. their slang
6. their work ethic
7. the way they treat each other
8. their priorities
9. their profanity
10. their piercings and tattoos
11. (often) their parents!!

5. If you're working with colleagues on this activity, this is the time to share circled items and ideas for positive influence actions. Listen to one another's plans. Take this opportunity to question, add thoughts and ideas, and encourage each other in your plans to influence the factors you can influence—and do it in a healthy, connective way.

6. Keep this **Attitude Inventory**. You'll use it again in the next two action steps.

Action Step 2.2   Change Your Self-Talk

Earlier in this chapter, I said that the one thing you CAN change is YOU (or your attitude or the way you look at something or act). The biases that disconnect us (teachers) from our students the most are probably those things we just cannot change. When confronted with these issues, all kinds of negative self-talk, rationalizations, explanations, stereo-types, and fears swirl around our brains. Negative self-talk conspires against connective interaction. It's hard to stop bad-mouthing the "offensive trait."

You can do this activity alone, but it is a lot more fun and productive if you do it with a group of colleagues. As you work together to challenge and change negative thoughts, you'll nurture adult relationships that provide support for the adults as you do a better job of connecting with the kids.

1. Review your **Attitude Inventory** from Action Step 2.1. Look at the items you did not circle. Those are the issues you admit you cannot influence. This action step pushes you to think about and write down your usual negative self-talk about these.

You've Gotta Connect

2. Becoming aware of the negative mental category is the first step. Mitigating its impact is the next. Choose one of the items you did not circle. Use the two-column form **Deconstructing the Mental Commentary** on page 70. Write the offending behavior or issue at the top.

3. In the left column, write the negative comments, criticisms, justifications, and arguments that run through your head— or that you say aloud to students or are tempted to say aloud. This is similar to the process my wife Penny and I followed when our son wanted the tattoo. Write it in quotes, just as it runs through your head or mouth!

4. Now comes the challenging part. In the right-hand column, try to flip each negative statement into a positive one. You might not be able to do this for each one. Your colleagues, however, can help by brainstorming possible responses.

5. Repeat this process for other offending items from your "can't influence" list.

6. Listen to the efforts of colleagues. This will absolutely breed significant compassion for those students and help you take giant steps toward connection.

7. Put your ideas to the test. Changing the negative talk running through your head will change the way you relate to students who have those annoying attitudes or passions you can't change.

Action Step 2.3 Give It a Rest!

In the last action step, you practiced a constructive way to deal with your own approach to some of those behaviors you find hardest to stomach. While you can't change their preference in friends or clothes, their hairstyles or piercings, you've started working on changing your attitude. But maybe you still struggle with the urges to change these things. Maybe you just can't resist the obsession with keeping them away from music you find offensive. Here's an idea that can work. I've seen it work with fellow teachers. It's helped me (yes—even tolerant me).

1. Go back to your **Attitude Inventory** from Action Step 2.1. Copy the list of items that are not circled. Put this list of "things I can't change" to rest. Destroy the list! You could wad it up and throw it away, but that is rather boring.

2. Get creative. Do something active and permanent. Why not burn the list or shred it? Fold it into a paper airplane and fly it somewhere. Create a social gathering with the colleagues (or even students) and hold a wake. Meet around a campfire and give brief eulogies before you cast your lists to the flames. In the process, you will relieve your mind of the burden of things out of your control. You will be free to react to these things in new ways.

Action Step 2.4 Up Close & Personal

You've examined some of your attitudes about this "crop" of students. These are generalized instincts, gripes, annoyances, or judgments about a generation or a whole subculture. Now it's time to focus on individuals. For the sake of time, we'll start with random choice of a few. I heartily encourage you, however, to look very closely at your biases toward **every student**—both favorable and unfavorable biases.

1. Randomly choose the names of nine students. You might do this by dropping a pencil or finger on your student roster with eyes closed. Or, have someone else choose them for you. Make yourself a code sheet somewhere, giving a number to each name.

2. Make a copy of the **Get Personal!** form on page 71. Write the number for each student at the top of one of the circles. You can write the students' names instead of a code number, but I suggest the code. You will be writing some personal opinions/biases about students, and it may not be a good idea to have a paper floating around with such information that someone can see associated with specific names.

3. For each name, write a phrase or sentence that describes at least one impression or bias you have about this student. Be honest, but do not over-think this. Include positive as well as negative impressions.

4. Go back to each circle. Ponder your bias. Label each one to get at the concept associated with your impression or what led to your bias. Here are some possible labels:

- appearance
- dress
- study habits
- family background or issues
- health
- peer choices
- language
- behavior
- ethnic background
- self concept

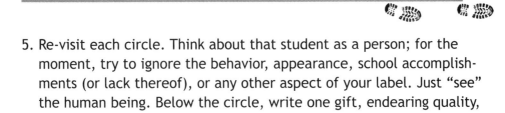

5. Re-visit each circle. Think about that student as a person; for the moment, try to ignore the behavior, appearance, school accomplishments (or lack thereof), or any other aspect of your label. Just "see" the human being. Below the circle, write one gift, endearing quality, dream, interest, human need, or talent. If this does not come easily, watch these students for a few days. Then complete the activity.

6. Follow this up by trying to identify your biases for every student with whom you interact. Get in the habit of trying to see past the bias and focus on a quality beneath the surface look, culture, or behavior. You'll be amazed at how differently you begin to feel about even the most troublesome students! This is a huge connective step!

Action Step 2.5 Environment Stealth Check

Try this one-week experiment to gauge how colleagues are doing at accepting students. You'll have to hang out in the teacher's lounge or lunchroom, faculty meetings, or other places where the adults in the school gather.

1. Starting tomorrow, or Monday, sharpen your hearing. Listen to the comments adults make about students. Every time you hear a statement about a student, make a mental note of whether it is positive or negative.

2. Use the **Comment Tally** form on page 72 to keep track of these comments. Certainly you hear a lot of commentary about students daily. Systematically record what is broadcast. Keep your chart handy, but definitely out of sight.

3. Don't let anyone know what you are doing. Most colleagues would be really miffed if they knew

you were keeping a tally of their statements to evaluate the environmental influence on student acceptance. This is not about evaluating individuals. If you are not able to leave individuals out of it, then do not attempt this task. (Also, if people know you are doing this, they will be on guard and not talk as normal. You want an honest inventory of your surroundings, which includes colleagues in their natural habitat.) Do not record any names or statements. Merely make a tally.

4. Do the math. Find the total number of tallies. Then divide the positive number by the total and the negative number by the total to find the percentage of each.

5. What do you do with this information? Evaluate how your work environment affects you. Record your thoughts to the prompts on page 73, **Response to Stealth-Check.**

Action Step 2.6
Repeat That, but Change the Subject

Now it's time to make **yourself** the subject. Investigate your own comments that show attitudes toward students.

1. For one week, do the same inventory you did in Action Step 2.5. (Use the **Comment Tally** form on page 72.) This time, limit the sample to your statements. Here is the tricky part: Now that you are recording your own statements, you'll probably become exceedingly conscious of what you say. You might catch yourself before you badmouth a kid. If that occurs, it would be (to quote my fellow Buckeye Neil Armstrong) "one giant leap for mankind."

2. At the end of the weeklong tally, tabulate the percentages of negative and positive comments.

3. Compare the results of Action Steps 2.5 and 2.6. If you find that you are more negative than the colleagues with whom you associate, quite frankly you have some work to do. If you find you are more positive, then you may just be a favorable influence on your crabby co-workers. You could become the change agent that your school needs. Or, you could be the person who is annoyingly in a better mood that everyone else.

4. Evaluate how your work environment affects you. Make a copy of page 73, **Response to Stealth-Check**. Write your responses to the prompts. Compare these with the same form you completed after your tally of your colleagues' comments.

5. Make a mental or actual list of negative comments that stood out—the ones you can't forget. Make another list of positive comments that stick in your mind. Resolve to use the positive comments and strike the negative ones from your conversations.

Action Step 2.7
Pardon Me, Your Biases Are Showing

It doesn't do much good for us to list our biases without examining how they play out. So on the last action step for this chapter, I suggest that you really look at yourself in the mirror (metaphorically). You'll consider how your attitudes translate into your behavior, and the kinds of messages that behavior gives to your students.

1. Go back and take a look at your initial **Attitude Inventory** that you created for Action Step 2.1. You wrote some "beliefs," gripes, biases, and such about this crop of students in general. (You can add to that list, if you have thought of more since then!)

2. Look at this list in a new light. Think about how each attitude or bias translates into things you do. For example, if you hate their manners, how do you communicate that, how do you behave in the presence of an exhibit of bad manners, or how do you respond (or not respond)? Or if a student dresses in a way that you accept, rather than abhor, how do you act?

3. Choose five of the items from that list (or include any other biases you have). Write these on a fresh list. You can use the **How Do My Biases Show?** form from page 74.

4. Do an honest reflection on the ways each bias shows. Think about your verbal responses and nonverbal responses. Think about how you show approval of student behavior on this issue as well as disapproval. Think about the messages your behavior gives to your students. Jot down these reflections.

5. Read this over. Share and discuss with colleagues. Ask for their feedback. I heartily suggest that you ask your students to give you feedback too. They are likely to be much more aware (and perhaps more honest) about how your attitudes translate into behavior.

ATTITUDE INVENTORY

This generation of kids! Here are the things about them
that I abhor (or, at the least, that annoy me, worry me,
disturb me, stymie me, or disgust me big time).

1 _____

2 _____

3 _____

4 _____

5 _____

6 _____

7 _____

8 _____

9 _____

10 _____

11 _____

12 _____

You've Gotta Connect

Deconstructing the Mental Commentary

*The Offending Issue or Behavior*_____

NEGATIVE MENTAL COMMENTARY   *CHALLENGE to the* **NEGATIVE COMMENTARY**

You've Gotta Connect   **70**

GET PERSONAL!

Randomly choose the names of nine students. Write the names
(or code numbers for the names) in the circles. Write at least one
gut reaction about or characterization for each student.

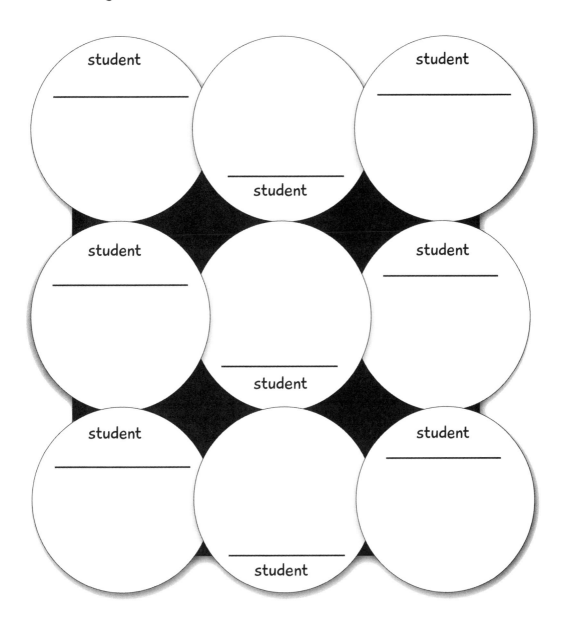

Comment Tally

Use simple tally marks ⫶⫶⫶⫶ II to record numbers of comments.

Dates:_____

_____
Total Positive Comments

_____
Total Negative Comments

_____
Total Comments

_____
% of Comments That Were Positive

_____
% of Comments That Were Negative

Response to Stealth-Check

Write your thoughts and answers to each question.

1. Did you hear more positive comments or more negative comments?

2. Are you surprised by the results (and why or why not?)

3. Are there venues in which you heard more negative comments? Which ones?

4. Are there any really positive venues in your school? Which ones?

5. Did you hear any comments similar to those you make yourself?

6. How did this activity affect you?

7. What emotions did you experience during this process?

8. What generalizations or "take-aways" can you describe from doing this process?

You've Gotta Connect

How Do My Biases Show?

Bias 1:

How I show it:

What it probably says to the student:

Bias 2:

How I show it:

What it probably says to the student:

Bias 3:

How I show it:

What it probably says to the student:

Bias 4:

How I show it:

What it probably says to the student:

Bias 5:

How I show it:

What it probably says to the student:

Learning Targets Checklist

To summarize what you have learned in this chapter, check ✓ if you . . .

_____ can identify your attitudes about your students' behaviors, attitudes, habits, or interests in general and describe which are connecting and which are disconnecting.

_____ can identify biases you have in favor of or against certain individual students.

_____ are able to explain how some of your biases translate into behavior toward students.

_____ can notice aspects of your environment that influence your attitudes and acceptance of students, and can describe those influences.

_____ can name some areas of nostalgia that endanger your ability to live and act in the present with current students.

_____ have admitted to yourself or others some areas where your attitudes about acceptance of students need to change.

_____ have an interest in letting go of some of the attitudes, patterns, environmental influences, or nostalgia that get in the way of accepting all your students.

_____ can verify that you have completed most of the Get-Connected Action Steps in this chapter.

You've Gotta Connect

Chapter 3

Communication

What You Say (and How You Say It) Matters

Big Joel was a powerful kid, well over 6 feet and well over 200 pounds. He was the star of our varsity football team—the kind of player that I wish I'd been back in high school. With the size, skill, intensity, and focus, he fit all my jock hero stereotypes. In those days, I coached football—though not the varsity team. While I didn't have the joy of coaching Big Joel, I was honored to have this Friday night hero in my study hall. It was a pleasure! He was outgoing. The boys looked up to him. The girls were crazy about him.

Ordinarily, I would have an easy and immediate connection with a kid like Big Joel. I was and am a big sports fan. I'd often approach him with sports talk. I mean, why not? He was a jock. I was a coach. Of course this is the topic on which such pairings converse—right? But my usual sports-centered connection didn't seem to work. When we interacted, it was cordial, but surface. Joel would respond politely, but the conversation was generally a dead end. I was puzzled.

Every day, I brought my newspaper to study hall and announced when I'd completed my reading. Students would swoop to my desk and pick it over like a discarded carcass. (This is quite unlike today's world wherein kids couldn't care less about a newspaper or even be able to identify one in a police lineup). One day I

76

noticed Joel rooting around in the remains of my newspaper. Only two sections were left—Arts & Entertainment, and remarkably, Sports. In wonder, I watched him pass over the sports page with zero interest. He then eagerly snatched the A&E section and returned to his desk with a jaunt in his step.

I was intrigued, so I ventured over and commented, "Wow, I'm really surprised you didn't snag the Sports section! I thought you'd want to read about the big game last night."

His response: "Oh don't worry Mr. Sturtevant. You've made that mistake many times. It doesn't bother me. I'm used to it. Everyone thinks I play sports because I'm obsessed with it like every other male in this school. I really don't find it that interesting. I kind of like playing, I'm good at it, and it might help me get into college. But otherwise, I could take it or leave it. I'd rather read about this new movie coming out."

I pushed my jaws shut, produced a complimentary smile, and humbly returned to my post.

What a bombshell! I never again related to Joel in the same way. I was never quite the same teacher again. Big Joel's lesson was a game changer for me. I'm glad I learned it early (though I need regular refresher courses). I try to get past my terms and my interests to their terms and their interests. And this, my friend, takes some investigative work!

The Pitch

You connect with students by communicating acceptance with what you say and how you say it. You can make great strides at the tasks of the last chapter, and I hope you do. You can acknowledge what you can't change; you can open your mind and heart to students; you can accept who they are. All is for naught if you can't **show** acceptance and connection to students—individually and as a group. For you, it might be habit, or fear, or old messages in your head that get in the way.

As for the students, they are masters at picking up the real story. They're keenly attuned to what you say, how you say it, and what you don't say. They can tell if you are genuinely interested in them as individuals. They can tell if you have biases against them as a group. Their razor-sharp detectors catch those implied messages lurking beneath your words. They know when you're real and when you are not. They know when you accept, judge, honor, dishonor, or disapprove. Kids learn these skills at a young age, or maybe they are born with them.

The adage "to know them is to love them" has great truth. You must know them in order to accept and connect. This chapter will help you learn new ways to know your students. It will also focus on ways to actively show that you embrace each one as a valued person, without pretending. For this chapter on **communicating acceptance**, your learning targets are:

Learning Targets

1. Get to know your students better as a group.

2. Get to know your students better as individuals.

3. Take new steps to hear and "read" your students' responses.

4. Recognize your verbal behaviors that show acceptance or non-acceptance.

5. Practice verbal behaviors that communicate acceptance and connection.

6. Develop new tools for showing that you accept students.

Put Yourself Out There

Do you want your students to know you accept them? Step up! Throw yourself into it! Get excited about showing that you want to be with them, that you like them, and that you're glad they are around! Literally, be "out there" among your students, visibly and actively showing them that relating to them is your top priority. Take every chance to give connecting, welcoming messages. The more positive, eager, and genuine signals you give to students, the better your relationships will be!

Here are some of the simple, easy messages to give:

While walking through the crowded hallway:

- Say hello to everyone (not enough time for "What's up?")—just "Hi!"

- Call out your students by name: "Hey young Leah!"

- If you want to say hello to a large group of students simultaneously, trill your l's in Espanol: "Heeeellllllllllo!" Accompany this with a sweeping arm gesture.

- Sing the songs they're singing back at them.

- Smile and nod to each student. (Many won't return the greeting but don't fret—mission accomplished!)

- Walk with great posture in a slow nonthreatening way. Again, smile. (I can't emphasize it enough.)

- Briefly mimic their dance moves. (Yes, you'll look ridiculous.)

- If a student is too far away to hear your voice, try to make eye contact and point at her or him with a broad smile.

When students are entering your class:

- "Hello!"

- "Great outfit!"

- "I've missed you over the last 23 hours!"

- "Are you getting taller?"
- "Wasn't that was a horrible call last night against the Buckeyes?"
- "I'm coming to your play tonight!"
- smile, smile, smile
- fist bump
- high five
- handshake
- any kind of bow
- hands together in prayer position, then nod
- the Vulcan "Live Long and Prosper" finger split

A student does something praiseworthy in class:

- "That blew me away!"
- "Love the creativity of that!"
- "Tell me more about your idea. It's fascinating!"
- "Could you teach me how to do that?"
- "Why do I bother teaching you? I feel like the student in this class-room!"
- dramatic slow clap
- exaggerated facial expressions showing surprise and glee
- smile with two thumbs up
- reverent bow in their direction

Get to Know Them

Students arrive in your class. You are, by definition, not "one of them." You don't need to and should not be "one of them." If you want to connect to them, however, they must immediately sense that you value them. Here's the first way to do this: Let them see you embrace the whole of who they are—what they like and dislike, what they do, what excites them, what they live for, and what their lives are like.

In 2007, Chuck Klosterman wrote a fascinating piece titled "Death by Harry Potter" for *Esquire* magazine. The writer confessed his cluelessness about the popular novel series and lamented about how this ignorance would probably cost him in the future when the 2007 teens grow up and take over. For teachers, Chuck's message is particularly poignant. Not only will cluelessness about current youth cultural references cost you in the future, but this obliviousness will cost you now—in a big way. How can you connect with students if you don't speak their language?

Obviously, youth trends change rapidly. When I first started teaching in 1985, all the cool girls wore stirrup pants or high-waisted jeans. Ten years later, the only females who wore stirrup pants were grandmas, and high-waisted jeans became "mom jeans." So while styles, music, movies, TV shows, and slang change, the presence of generation gaps does not. It only widens. Back in 1985, I was only a few years older than my high school seniors. Because our generational references were similar, I totally understood them. I could quote their shows, sing their music, and even bust out their dance moves. Time marches on. Now I'm older than many of their parents. It's *The Picture of Dorian Gray* in reverse. The teachers age. The students do not.

As I sat monitoring Saturday School on April 6, 2013, (yes 1980's teens, it's just like *The Breakfast Club*), I decided to enlist my captive audience in a job. Together, we went to work creating a tool to assess a teacher's awareness of current teen or pre-teen culture. Here's the result: "The 2013 Teacher Marginal Propensity to Remain Hip Scale." (The kids tell me that no one says "hip" any more. I changed it to "cool.") I'll need a new assessment next year! Take the survey right now.

You've Gotta Connect

2013 TEACHER'S MARGINAL-PROPENSITY-TO-REMAIN-~~HIP~~ Cool SCALE

Apply the flowing slang terms to the matching situation:

A. PHOTOBOMB

B. EPIC FAIL

C. NOOB

D. PWNED

E. POS

F. SICK

G. HATER

H. TROLLING

_____1. The teacher is totally clueless about current youth cultural references.

_____2. I can't text what I want right now because I'm being watched.

_____3. Oh, that's actually quite outstanding.

_____4. Thanks to him, my instagram post is ruined.

_____5. He just got defeated by a hated adversary.

_____6. They're broadcasting malicious lies.

_____7. I can't believe he screwed up that amazingly easy task.

NAME EACH MOVIE DESCRIBED BELOW:

8. The graduates of East Great Falls High School get back together.

9. Tobey Maguire suits up again.

10. After six months, the girls finally identify the song.

11. This disturbing movie is about teen partying and features the drug dealer, T-Rick.

12. These girls can sing a capella.

13. This is based on a cheesy 1987 TV show.

14. Andrew Detmer develops his mental capacities to a shocking degree.

IDENTIFY THE NAME OF THE CHARACTER AND THE TV SHOW:

15. This young woman seems dumber than she really is, at least compared to her science nerd neighbors.

16. This short, husky, Hispanic adolescent enjoys the finer things in life. Unfortunately, he is far too cool for middle school.

17. If you sing well enough, you may just get this handsome, voluminously tatted, white tee-shirt wearing evaluator to turn around and look at you.

18. This spiritual middle school teacher sports beautiful dark brown bangs, big blue eyes, and a compassionate disposition, which is helpful in dealing with her three un-evolved male roommates.

19. The objective of this alpha female bail bondswoman is to free Storybrooke, Maine, from ignorance.

20. This patriarch and pawn shop co-owner is busy haggling with customers over the selling price of various historical artifacts.

WHO SINGS THE FOLLOWING?

21. Thrift Shop

22. Harlem Shake

23. Suit & Tie

24. When I Was Your Man

25. Stay

26. Just Give Me a Reason

27. Started from the Bottom

28. Feel This Moment

29. Love Me

30. I Knew You Were Trouble

Answers:
1. C, 2. E (parents over shoulder), 3. F, 4. A, 5. D, 6. G, 7. B, 8. *American Reunion*, 9. *The Amazing Spider-Man*, 10. *The Perks of Being a Wallflower*, 11. *Project X*, 12. *Pitch Perfect*, 13. *21 Jump Street*, 14. *Chronicle* , 15. Penny from *The Big Bang Theory*, 1. Manny from *Modern Family*, 17. Adam Levine from *The Voice*, 18. Jess from *New Girl*, 19. Emma from *Once Upon a Time*, 20. Richard "Old Man" Harrison from *Pawn Stars*, 21. Macklemore & Ryan Lew Mikky is (featuring Wanz), 22. Baauer, 23. Justin Timberlake (featuring Jay-Z), 24. Bruno Mars, 25. Rihanna (featuring Ekko), 26. Pink (featuring Nate Ruess), 27. Drake , 28. Pitbull (featuring Christina Aguilera), 29. Lil Wayne (featuring Drake and Future), 30. Taylor Swift

When you're done, share your results with your students. They'll love it! (You can find the answers on page 83.) Make sure you try the **Get-Connected Action Step 3.1** later in this chapter. It's a process for getting your students to create their own tool to assess teacher awareness of their culture.

Do make time to become literate in the culture of your students. How well do you know this generation? Ask yourself these questions (and others like them):

- Can you name their favorite songs?
- Can you hum some of those tunes or sing a few bars (if the words are appropriate)?
- Can you name and describe hottest performance artists they love?
- Do you understand their slang?
- Do you use some current slang, when appropriate?
- Do you know who their heroes or icons are?
- Do you have an idea of how those heroes influence your students?
- Do you understand their methods of communication, including electronic?
- Are you aware who is in what clique or group in the class or school?
- Do you have a feel for what they watch on TV, what apps they have on their phones and tablets, and what games are hot right now?
- Can you identify most of the interests, activities, needs, or stresses that compete with schoolwork for their attentions and passions?
- Do you have a feel for the kinds of social pressures they face?
- Can you name and explain what scares them?

- Could you describe what it is like to be a 12-year old or 16-year old (or whatever age you teach) in your town, in your school, in today's world?

If you can answer "yes" to many of these questions, you can use the understandings as you interact with students. Did you answer "no" to most of them? Then you have some work to do. If they see you working to know about their whole lives, students will see that you care about them.

Don't start getting anxious! Note that I did **not** say you have to **like** their music. I did **not** say you should **dress** like their favorite rock star. (Please don't!) I did **not** say you have to **approve** of their choices. I'm encouraging you to honor them by knowing about their world and acknowledge that you know some stuff about them without showing judgment.

As you work to know what they're about, find things you can approve. Show this by such behaviors as . . .

- making a comment about a movie they're all seeing

- sending out a fun text

- showing some excitement about an icon they love

- keeping up on the latest developments on a TV show they watch

- joking (lovingly) about a fashion fad

- breaking into the lyrics of one of the hit raps

- talking about bullying, playground terrors, their work load, and other things that worry them

Student cultural references and preferences **do** seem like a foreign language. There's a big difference between being conversational and fluent in their language. For myself, I figure that if I am conversational it means

I can function, not at a high level, but enough to survive. (After all, tourists need to know how to ask: "Where's the restroom?" or "How much for this?" And naivety can lead to exploitation or at least discomfort.)

I don't claim to be fluent in "teenagerese," or "pre-teenagerese," but I know it is critical to have some understanding of what they say and do. So get acquainted! When you show actions such as those in the lists above, even the smallest ones, you connect with students. These actions show you care enough to pay attention to their world, even if it pulls you a bit out of your comfort zone to do so.

Get to the One-on-One

So you've greeted students in the hallway, welcomed them to your room, and praised them in class. But connecting is more than gestures and simple acknowledgments. Connecting implies relationships. You've just opened the door a crack and looked inside. Now, you have to enter.

Go to the trouble; try to get to know each student. Just the effort shows them that you care. **Within a few weeks of walking into your class (or sooner), each student needs to know you have noticed him or her.** This is at the core of the art of connection, and is the heart of this chapter. One-on-one interactions accelerate the connection process. Even if you have 150 different students, this is not as big a job as it may seem. There are dozens of possibilities each day for personal interactions.

You could help a student with his assignment, have a short chat with her before class, share a laugh with him in the hallway, counsel her when she is upset, ask him how he's doing on a goal he has set, or call out

86

a friendly greeting to her at the grocery store. These are small build-ing blocks to stronger relationships. The most natural way to focus on individuals is to have casual conversations with as many students as possible as often as possible. Invariably, this will lead to learning many things about them. I like to greet a student, let him or her see that I'm paying attention, then ask, "How's it going?" or "What's up?" These may seem like vacant questions. But actually they are great. Students learn quickly that I'm not asking just as a greeting, expecting no real answer. They see me lean in and wait for a response. They learn that I am truly seeking to connect. I'm amazed at the honest and substantive answers students give!

Class projects or group work sessions are rich venues for personal con-nections. While kids work on research or presentations, I walk around and check their progress. Of course, this is an important part of the teaching process. But it is also a fine segue to connection. This gives me a chance to chat about their weekend plans, favorite hangouts, latest video game craze, what TV show they watched last night, who they think will win the big game this weekend, what they plan to do after school, or with whom they'll spend time after school. As I question them, I monitor their nonverbal signals. If someone is open and animat-ed, I see a green light and I push forward with the connection. If he is closed and hesitant, I get a yellow caution signal. I back off and wait for another opportunity in the future to connect.

Listen to Students

Here's a scenario that might happen to you:

A few weeks into the school year or semester, you're pleased with your outreach efforts. The majority of your class is receptive. They respond enthusiastically to your greetings. They laugh at your jokes. They share stories and start conversations. They eagerly participate in class.

A teacher who wants to connect to me listens and keeps the conversation between us.

You've Gotta Connect

Most likely, there's another, smaller group that seems willing to bond. They're reserved, but you can sense they're warming to you, and it's just a matter of time. It would be easy to pat yourself on the back and think, "job well done."

But not so fast! There's another small cadre of kids, perhaps just a handful, that seem withdrawn. Some even seem hostile. Okay, you signed on to be a teacher. Roll up your sleeves, put your ego on hold, and accept the challenge of melting these arctic exteriors. You may not win all of them over, but you'll succeed with many—a remarkable accomplishment. However, you'll have zero conversions if you're too intimidated to try.

The 3 P's: In my relationship quest, I have found it helpful to repeat the 3P mantra frequently: Keep prying. Keep persisting. Be patient.

▪ *Keep prying.*

> This may sound negative, but it is actually positive. It is gentle, focused nudging of a reluctant student toward being comfortable enough to open up a bit. Inquisitive teachers who are not too pushy have the best chance of bonding with the unwilling. Please keep at it! You never know when you'll have a breakthrough. You could start with the exercises in **Get-Connected Action Step 3.2** found later in this chapter. It's a questionnaire that invites students to begin to let you know some things about them.

▪ *Keep persisting.*

> Find out what the reluctant student values. Do this through close observation and gentle "prying." Once you're aware of the passions, you can learn something about them, if not engage in them. (Stick to passions that are legal and ethical for you to discuss with the students.) After you develop a journeyman's knowledge of drawing, skateboarding, tattooing, rap music, or video games, you can impress the student with intelligent questions and openness. If the going is rough, don't be discouraged.

It's tough getting the cold shoulder from anyone, particularly when you're trying so hard. Think of the crabby youngster as **your teacher**. ("What?" you ask! Your reaction to their miserable attitudes teaches you a lot about yourself. You'll learn how you deal with difficult people—a valuable lesson!)

- *Be patient.*
  Embrace bonding with your students as a process—perhaps long and at times painful or awkward. If you come on too strong at the beginning, they'll experience you as a creepy stalker instead of a caring mentor. Be cool! You have time, perhaps all year. The goal is to have a strong relationship as soon as possible, but accept that it may not happen until late in the game.

To build relationships with students as a group or individually, you **do** have to work at it. It must be a conscious commitment. You can't be hiding behind your desk or buried in your grading databases. You have to be available, open, watchful, alert, and engaged—seizing every opportunity to connect. Try **Get-Acquainted Action Step 3.3** later in this chapter. This suggests a way to keep on track with one-to-one connections with your students.

Watch What You Say

A teacher's words have the power to connect or disconnect. Your words can nurture, uplift, encourage, honor, and instruct. They can diminish, harm, injure, put down, or discourage. Scrutinize what you say; this is a huge part of showing students you accept them. Also, find out what messages students receive from your words. As teachers, most of us need a lot of thought, plenty of practice, and some serious feedback in order to make the best use of our words.

Consider these familiar scenarios.

- Scenario 1:

  What the teacher says: *Now this time . . . you need to apply yourself!*
  What the student hears: *You're a slacker.*
  VS.
  What the teacher says: *With this assignment, you're going to suc-ceed. I'll help you every step of the way!*
  What the student hears: *You can do this. I'll work hard to see that you do. You can count on me.*

- Scenario 2:

  What the teacher says: *You look nice for a change.*
  What the student hears: *Ordinarily, you dress like a hood.*
  VS.
  What the teacher says: *You look nice today; solid ensemble!*
  What the student hears: *You clean up well.*

- Scenario 3:

  What the teacher says: *Are you late again?*
  What the student hears: *As usual, you're up to no good.*
  VS.
  What the teacher says: *Why were you late? Talk to me.*
  What the student hears: *I get that you probably have a good reason for being late. Is there a problem? I'd like to help.*

So many words, comments, phrases have the ability to break connec-tions with students. Unfortunately, a thoughtless comment can set back a connection you've worked hard to build. On the other hand, words are wonderful connectors and healers when used well. Be alert to words that hurt or disconnect. Build your repertoire of words that connect.

Teacher Talk That Disconnects

- *What did I just tell you?*
- *Where were you when I explained this?*
- *Do you know where your seat is?*
- *While we're waiting for your answer, the polar ice caps are melting.*
- *If I were you...*
- *I like the way Brad is working (listening, behaving)...*
- *This isn't brain surgery.*
- *There you go again!*
- *Did you or did you not read the assignment?*
- *That's not a good excuse.*
- *I've had enough of that attitude.*
- *You're late...again.*
- *You always...*
- *You never...*
- *Some of us don't like this.*
- *The last class seemed to get this without any trouble.*
- *That's a terrible excuse.*

Teacher Talk That Connects

- *You decide.*
- *Next time, could you....*
- *How could you look at this differently?*
- *I never thought of that idea.*
- *I see where you're coming from.*
- *Would you like more time to think about this?*
- *Say some more.*
- *Thanks for taking a risk.*
- *What's your opinion?*
- *Can you tell me more?*
- *I think you can handle this.*
- *What's your idea for how to solve this?*
- *Would you like my help?*
- *How do you see this?*
- *Thanks for sharing your idea.*
- *Does anyone have a different answer?*

Try **Get-Connected Action Step 3.4** later in this chapter. This will push you to listen to yourself and examine the signals your words project to students.

Watch How You Say It

Recently, I posted a YouTube clip of the old R&B group the Brothers Johnson and their song *Stomp*. To my delight, a long-lost friend saw it and tracked me down on Facebook. I hadn't heard from her in 20 years! Back in high school, we were huge R&B fans. She told me that this great song brought back wonderful memories. As an aside, she confided that her 15-year-old son watched the video and was not impressed. He thought it very cheesy, and I am certain most modern teens would agree.

I sent her back this message: "Kids!" I meant that young people today just don't understand what they are missing. It was as if my arms were folded across my chest, and I was shaking my head in disbelief.

She couldn't see my body language of course. And she could not hear my intended emphasis and tone: **Kids!**

When she wrote back and told me about her children, I realized she had misunderstood my statement. She read my statement as: "I didn't know you had children," probably picturing me wide-eyed with palms exposed asking the question with the emphasis on last part of the word: **Kids?**

> ## Ask Yourself:
>
> *Do I talk too fast, too loud? Do I yell? Do I have annoying habits?*

Most of us have been told (or said), "Don't take that tone with me!" or "It is not what you said, it was your tone!" There is so much more to verbal communication than the actual words. Often, the **way** something is said transmits a more powerful (or vastly different) message than the words.

92

Tone of voice is the manner of speaking or the quality of the voice. Tone has many aspects. It includes emphasis (on words or syllables), pace, pitch, volume, and a host of other characteristics. Someone's tone can be nervous, full, hushed, uncertain, arrogant, slurred, abrupt, tentative, sassy, sarcastic, and on and on. It can betray your attitude, underlying emotions, or confidence level. There are a lot of subtleties to the topic of tone!

For teachers, tone awareness is crucial as it plays a major role in communication. It has a power you may not realize. Tone betrays emotions and attitudes. If you are not careful, your message is totally lost, or the wrong message is signaled, or a message that you had hoped to disguise is projected. Many of us don't even notice our tones of voice. But trust me, students **do.** They pick up all kinds of signals. **Manage your tone.** This will be a valuable tool in forging strong connections and communicating respect and care to your students.

Now granted, my Facebook message exchange was a harmless misunderstanding. It did not pose a risk of something as critical as breaking a relationship or starting a war. (Misunderstood messages can have effects that devastating, though.) The example did remind me of the power of tone. And it does alert me to the difficulty of communicating effectively in e-mails or texts. Something is lost in the absence of the sound of the voice and accompanying nonverbal expressions. Even the all-caps and the multiple exclamation points DON'T QUITE SUBSTITUTE for the face-to-face communication!!!!!

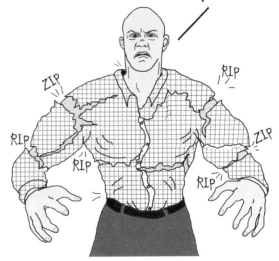

Don't you kids know that I care about you?

Author's Reflection

It was the spring of 1986, and I was winding down my first year as a public school teacher. It was a wonderful experience, but to be honest with you, I was running out of steam. I was not sure if I could make it through the whole month of May. My biggest challenge was my last-period class-from-hell. Looking back, I know that I was totally responsible for the condition of that class. I got along with the kids well, but they controlled the class. My lesson plans, which worked well in other classes, just fizzled out a while before the end of that last-period. That left a chunk of dead time; that time felt like a satanic cocktail.

I was never so glad to see June. When it finally came, I looked back to evaluate my year. I felt good about everything but that seventh-period class. "Why? What went wrong?" I asked myself. Then I had a eureka! moment. It was my anxiety. I was always apprehensive before that class. There was something about that group of kids that shook my confidence. Also, there was something about the atmosphere of the last period class. Out of nervousness, I presented the lesson and went through the activities at lightning speed. I got on autopilot and rushed through everything. I think that, subconsciously, I was afraid to take a breath—for fear a nanosecond would leave room for them to self-destruct or wrest any remaining control from me. I'm sure I was drowning. I know I was disconnected. I ran out of things to say before the end of class. Of course, I had not a clue about how to do something productive with an unruly bunch of high school kids in any leftover time. (Where was I during my teacher training courses? Did I never hear anything about holding a discussion, or getting feedback, or helping students reflect, or having a meaningful and relaxed conversation with a group of students?)

*I was the **real** student in that class. My students, through what one might label misbehavior, taught me what not to do. (If any former students from that class are reading this, please accept my apologies for not being much of a teacher and my appreciation for your lessons to me.) From that point on, I was alert to that kind of anxiety. I spoke more slowly and deliberately. I paid attention to the students, listening and watching for their signals and feedback. I took time to see that they were engaged in the lesson. It worked like magic. There was no mayhem at the end of the class. The students got better instruction, I was far more connected to the students, and the next year that last "class from hell" period became one my favorites.*

This discovery brought an unexpected bonus. The discipline in my classes took a huge, positive leap. The chaos I feared did not break out during lessons, even in the more difficult-to-manage groups. Yes, I had eliminated the "idle-hands-are-the-devil's-workshop" dead time at the end of class. More than that, my demeanor had changed. I found that when I spoke in a calm, confident but animated voice, students were more involved and attentive. Once I stopped the nervous yammering, I projected fewer negative, nonverbal signals. As my confidence grew, teaching became a magical profession for me. Much of the change came from simple attention to my verbal style.

Pay attention to your words. Are you saying what you mean? Record some classes. What patterns do you hear? Ask your colleagues or teammates to reflect back to you the words and tone they overhear—both those that affirm students, and those that disconnect. Work through **Get-Connected Action Steps 3.6 and 3.7** later in this chapter. These exercises give you a chance to examine how tone of voice affects the listener and changes your interactions.

Notice What They Hear

Nobody knows better what messages you broadcast than those kids sitting in your class or walking past you in the hall. So the best way to improve at communicating acceptance is to ask the students what they hear. Do I need to repeat that? **Ask the students.** Yes, this takes courage. But I think you know I am right. They're the ones who can best teach you.

How do you learn what messages the students receive from you?

1. **Observe their responses.**
   Watch for times they flinch, smile, roll their eyes, pull back, wince, look proud, look hurt, relax, or close off.

2. **Listen to them.**
   Students say plenty. Some of it is directed at you. Some of it is not. Keep your ears open. Do they groan, grunt, or whisper to a neighbor? Do they sigh with relief, laugh, or make approving noises? What comments do they make about other teachers (that you can apply to yourself, or that you are sure they also say about you)? Listen to their direct responses to you. Are these comfortable, guarded, suspicious, reluctant, fearful, eager, or trusting?

3. **Ask them directly.**
   Yes, just stick out your neck, swallow your pride, open your mind, and ask what they are hearing. Try some
   questions like this:

   - What kinds of things do I say that feel respectful or accepting to you?

   - What do I say that is most obnoxious?

   - What do I say that puts you off?

   - What do I say that makes you feel smart (or welcome, or valued)?

Ask Yourself:

What do I say that causes my students to roll their eyes?

- Are there any things I say that make you feel I think you are stupid?
- Can you mimic examples of my tone of voice that give non-accepting (or accepting) signals?

There are dozens of questions you can ask. Work at establishing the kind of trusting communication that allows students to give you feedback. This can be done! Handled respectfully, you are not asking them to trash you. Instead, you show that you are genuinely interested in knowing about signals that disconnect. Try **Get-Connected Action Step 3.5** later in this chapter. You'll find out how to learn from students about the signals you project.

More Words About Words

We want to show students that they are accepted. With that goal in mind, I share a few more thoughts and experiences related to the things teachers say. Add the ideas below to your awareness list. Then work through **Get-Connected Action Step 3.8. It** will pull your attention toward some patterns you'll want to put on your no-no list and turn your energy toward some "yes-yes" goals.

You're Being Watched

You may think that students care little about what you say. Wrapped up in their own social needs and peer world, they may seem to ignore you. Well, it certainly is true that you're hardly the center of their world. Nevertheless, kids are amazing multilisteners.

Remember, this is the generation that can play a video game, text, watch a TV show, listen to an iPod, surf the Internet, and do homework—all at the same time. So be aware: Students hear what you say to other teachers, about other teachers, to parents, about parents, to other students, and about other students. Strong messages about your attitude and acceptance leak out when you gossip, converse casually, confront others, or talk on the phone.

Be Wary of Needy Messages

- "Wasn't that a great lesson?"

- "I spent all weekend preparing this cool activity for you."

- "I need you to be quiet."

- "Your behavior makes me sad."

- "I'm so displeased with these test scores."

Do I try to elicit compliments from my students?

You may not be this obvious. But there are many subtle ways that a teacher fishes for compliments or affirmation or asks students to meet his or her emotional needs. It is not your students' jobs to take care of you emotionally or make you feel capable, young, or attractive. Relish their freely given compliments and cooperation. **Avoid extracting these from them.** It is uncomfortable for your students and will send them into retreat. Be on the alert for times you might do this. Ask colleagues to give you feedback. Be a confident mentor for your students, not an insecure adult.

Protect Students

Never say anything to embarrass a student in front of peers. Never back a student into a corner and have her lose face. On the contrary, be alert to ways to help a student save face in front of peers. Discipline students privately—not in front of classmates. Likewise, protect students from embarrassing praise. There is a flood of research and advice available these days about appropriate praise. The rule of thumb is to praise effort in a way that boosts confidence—instead of praising the person or the accomplishment itself. Every time you protect a student from exposure to peer derision, judgment, ridicule, or shame, you make great strides in real connection with that student.

Make a Pact

If you have not already done something like this, make a pact right now with yourself (and silently, with your students) to get rid of words and expressions that disconnect. This means words and expressions, responses or comments that blame, shame, threaten, discount, humiliate, belittle, bribe, preach, label, discriminate, or disrespect a student (or anyone else).

Be Polite

This, simply, covers it all. Speak kindly (no yelling) and respectfully.

This chapter has focused on how to show students you value and accept them. The path to this goal includes continued awareness of what you've been doing and saying, commitment to drop disconnecting habits, and plans to nurture more connecting patterns. Make strides toward this goal with the Get-Connected Action Steps that follow. Then, don't neglect to finish the chapter by summarizing what you learned in the chapter. See the **Learning Targets Checklist** on the final page of Chapter 3.

Get-Connected! Action Steps

Action Step 3.1 Cultural Literacy Checkup

If you want to connect with students, you must tune in to their culture to a respectable level. By *respectable*, I mean to a level that students can read as interested and accepting. I can't think of any better way to measure this than to ask the students to set the rating scale.

1. Ask students to create a questionnaire that measures teacher awareness of the students' culture. Explain that they should generate questions or statements to finish or use any other written approach. The purpose is to tap into what the teacher "gets" about their interests, habits, passions, and activities or about the things that influence them. Ask them to confine the questions to things they think adults who work with kids their age should know. Students might work in pairs or small groups to generate questions. If they are of fifth grade age or older, they should be able to do this process on their own. They'll need to find a way to fine tune the collected ideas to a survey that is of manageable length. Remind them to include only school-appropriate ideas and language.

2. Ask students how they'd like to review and share the results and how they'd like to respond. (For example, they may want to host a crash course on pre-teen life or suggest things for you to watch, try, or do to increase your literacy.) In any case, encourage some follow-up and feedback to you.

3. Pay attention to students' feedback. Use it to set goals for yourself. Set a timeline for students to check up on your progress. They will probably love to develop a second questionnaire to see how you're coming along.

Note: Keep this process within your own classroom. Don't suggest that students give the questionnaire to other teachers, unless other teachers hear about it and ask to try it.

Action Step 3.2 Invitation to Connection

A survey is one way you can begin to gather some information about your students as individuals.

1. Use the survey **I'd Like to Know** on page 107, or design a questionnaire of your own. Ask questions, or provide sentences for students to finish. The goal is to learn a bit about each student without being too invasive.

2. Give students time to complete the survey thoughtfully. Assure them that the information is only for you and will not be shared with anyone else unless they wish it to be shared. Tell them they are free to skip any questions that they are not comfortable answering. (You might also tell them that they are free to amend the survey at any time. A student might wish they had answered differently, or want to add something later, particularly to the last two questions.)

3. Find a way to file away, mentally or otherwise, some key points about each student. Refer back to this information and use it to help you understand and connect with individuals. Keep these sheets in a private place.

Action Step 3.3 How Do I Know You?

As you get to know students, make use of what you learn to deepen relationships. Do this as opportunities present themselves. Also do this in a planned, purposeful way. This activity helps you check up on yourself to see that you **do** know things about each student and push yourself to relate to individuals.

1. Use the **Face to Face** form on page 108 to list student names. If you have several classes, prepare a form for each class. (You could create such a form on your computer instead.)

2. A few weeks into the year or semester, take time to write something in the second column that you have learned about each student. If you can't think of anything, use something from the surveys you used in Action Step 3.2. Then, jot down an idea for a comment or question you will ask the student. This gives you a plan for using what you know to make a connection.

3. Follow through. Write the date that you made the connection. You might want to set a target date for completing contacts with all the students.

Action Step 3.4 What Do I Really Say?

Now that you've read the ideas and examples in this chapter, you've got some food for thought about how you show acceptance to students (or how you show something else).

1. Think back over the past week, recalling responses to and communications with students. Think about your words, phrases, questions, and tones. Think about how these responses showed your acceptance or non-acceptance of an individual or group. (In the next chapter, we will focus on your nonverbal communication, such as body language.)

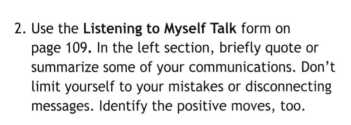

2. Use the **Listening to Myself Talk** form on page 109. In the left section, briefly quote or summarize some of your communications. Don't limit yourself to your mistakes or disconnecting messages. Identify the positive moves, too.

3. For each verbal communication you list, add a comment about what message you think was projected to an individual student or group of students.

4. Read back through this. Make some notes about what you learned from doing this task. Then hang onto this form. In Action Step 3.5, you'll have a chance to get some student feedback on your work here.

Action Step 3.5 What Do My Students Hear?

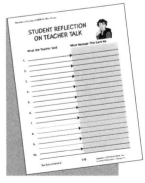

Take the evaluation of your verbal messages to the next level. This exercise asks students to tell you what they hear.

1. Use the **Student Reflection on Teacher Talk** form on page 110. Make a copy for each student, or project the page for students to use as a model.

You've Gotta Connect

2. Explain to students that you'd like them to reflect on expressions, comments, or words they hear you say. They should jot them down. For each one, they'll note what message or signal they get from the words. Clarify that you are looking for "talk" or tonal qualities that they might find either connecting or disconnecting.

3. Find time for students to share their observations with you in some way. Listen with an open mind. Take notes. Include this in a conversation with students about verbal signals people broadcast—signals that may be conscious or unconscious, intended or not. Talk about the idea that people often don't recognize these behaviors in themselves.

4. Share the reflections you gathered from completing the **Listening to Myself Talk** form from Action Step 3.4. Ask students if they got the messages you thought they might have received from some of your comments.

5. Your students might like the chance to do the same exercise you did in Action Step 3.4 using the **Listening to Myself Talk** form. They can use the form to do some self-reflection. Then, they could ask peers (or even you) to help them add to their lists.

Action Step 3.6 Hone In on Tone

It's not easy to hear how we sound to others. Most of us don't go around asking our students, family members, colleagues, or friends, "How is my tone of voice?" or "How do I come across to others verbally?" (Sometimes our family members tell us anyway—especially our own children.) Yet these are precisely the kinds of questions we need to ask.

1. Create a tone interview speed-date circuit to get honest reflections about your own tonal behavior. Gather some trusted friends, rela-

tives, colleagues, or students who have seen you make presentations or watched you in conversations. Arrange them in a circle.
Quickly move from one to the other. When you stand in front of a
person, it is his or her turn to give you one comment of positive
feedback about your tone of voice and one comment of "improvement needed" feedback. Use this information to summarize your
own strengths and weaknesses.

2. Work with trusted colleagues to move your tone
   quest to the arena of a presentation or discussion. Take turns listening in on a lesson. Or set up
   a discussion between two parties on a subject of
   high interest to both. Use the form **Tone Quest** on
   page 111 to record impressions of one speaker's
   tone. (If you are not able to do this with others,
   you could record one of your own discussions or
   presentations and listen to it later.) Trade places
   so that all parties are rated on the Tone Quest
   form. Find time to discuss the results and use
   them to identify tonal characteristics.

Action Step 3.7 Anxiety Check

Is there an interaction that causes you anxiety? It might be presenting to a particular class, dealing with a particular student, working
with an intense colleague or administrator, or having a conference
with an aggressive parent. Practice this the next time you find yourself in an anxiety-laden situation:

1. Deliberately slow the pace of everything you say. Don't step on
   the gas if the situation gets tense. Keep it slow and controlled.

You've Gotta Connect

2. When you are done, reflect on the experience. Ask yourself these questions:
   - *How did the slower pace affect my emotions?*
   - *Did the other person(s) take me more seriously than in other such situations?*

3. The next time you interact with that class or individual, notice how they respond to you. Do you see or feel any differences?

Action Step 3.8   Take Affirmative Action

At the end of this chapter about showing acceptance, it's time to set some goals for your own action.

1. Start with the **Words to Stamp Out!** form on page 112. Use it as a place to summarize some of what you learned about verbal connection and disconnection. Think about what stands out in your own behavior. Review your results from the previous action steps. For each of the talk balloons on the form, choose up to five items (words, phrases, tones, or habits) that you want to drop from your verbal repertoire with students.

2. Flip over the page and write two goals for affirmative action as alternatives to each of the above habits. Make this your "Yes-Yes" list!

3. Keep this list in a visible place as a reminder. Share it with your students, if you wish. They will help hold you accountable. Check back in a month to see how you are doing at replacing disconnecting talk with affirmative actions.

Welcome to this class! **I'd like to know** more about you.
Please complete any of the items with information you are willing to share.

Who is important to you?_____

What is your favorite movie?_____

Who are your heroes?_____

What is your greatest talent or gift?_____

What are your hobbies?_____

Where do you like to hang out?_____

What have you recently watched more than once on YouTube?

_____

What social medium or mediums do you prefer?

_____

What do you watch on TV?

_____

How do you spend your free time?_____

What is your favorite reading material?_____

What are you most passionate about?_____

What do you like most about yourself?_____

What is the most important thing about yourself
that you'd like your teachers to know?_____

Is there anything else you'd like this teacher to know?_____

Face to Face

Student	Something Personal I Know	Comment I Will Make	√ Done

LISTENING TO MYSELF TALK

What I Said

The Message This Probably Projected

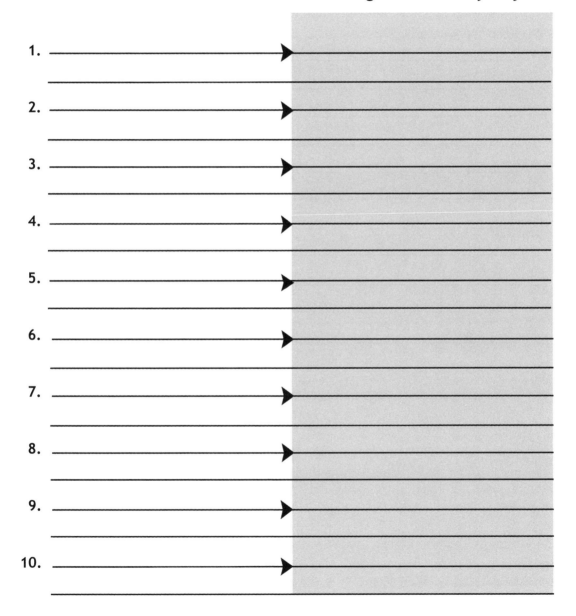

1.

2.

3.

4.

5.

6.

7.

8.

9.

10.

You've Gotta Connect

STUDENT REFLECTION ON TEACHER TALK

What the Teacher Said

What Message This Gave Me

1. _____

_____

2. _____

_____

3. _____

_____

4. _____

_____

5. _____

_____

6. _____

_____

7. _____

_____

8. _____

_____

9. _____

_____

10. _____

_____

Tone Quest

As you listen to a presentation or one person's part of an interchange,
reflect on what you noticed about the speaker's tone.

In 1-3, circle one choice. Then answer the two questions for each.

| nervous | **1. Volume** | too high | too low | just right | passionate |

nervous
imaginative
preachy
threatening
warm
soothing
reassuring
nasal
exuberant
boring
respectful
engaging
nurturing
unimaginative
arrogant
self-righteous

1. Volume   too high   too low   just right

How did this affect your comprehension?

How did this affect your receptivity?

2. Pitch   too high   too low   just right

How did this affect your comprehension?

How did this affect your receptivity?

3. Pace   too fast   too slow   just right

How did this affect your comprehension?

How did this affect your receptivity?

passionate
instructive
belittling
sarcastic
superior
uncertain
needy
choppy
hushed
humble
tentative
polite
denigrating
conversational
authoritative
authentic
encouraging

4. Write a description of other tonal aspects for the speaker. Choose
   from the words shown, or add any other words.

5. How did the tone, as you've described it, affect your comprehension
   of the subject?

6. How did these aspects of the speaker's tone affect your receptivity to
   the message or information?

You've Gotta Connect

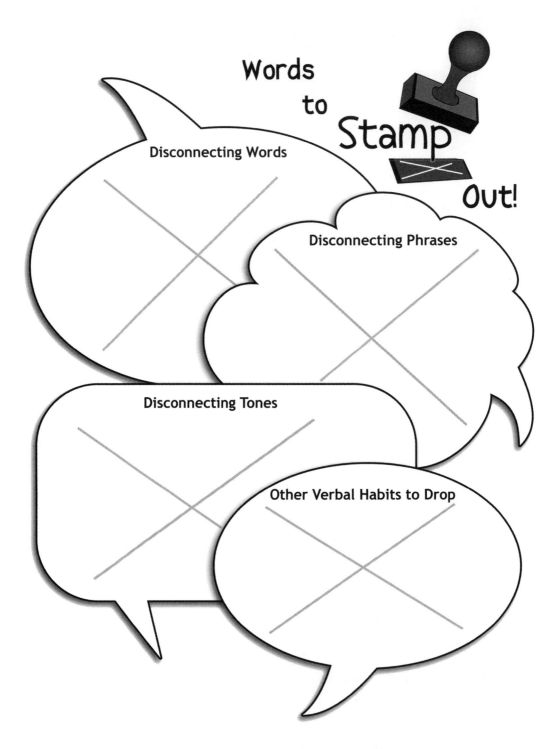

Words to Stamp Out!

Disconnecting Words

Disconnecting Phrases

Disconnecting Tones

Other Verbal Habits to Drop

Learning Targets Checklist

To summarize what you have learned in this chapter,
check ✓ if you . . .

_____ have significantly increased the number of individual
contacts and conversations with each student.

_____ can show that you've raised your level of literacy related to the culture of your students.

_____ can describe a few personal interests or gifts of each of
your students.

_____ remember several examples of feedback students have
given regarding your positive and negative verbal signals.

_____ are able to name at least five expressions or comments
that you have learned show acceptance to students,
and thus you will keep using them.

_____ are able to name at least five expressions or comments
that you have re-examined and replaced with more accepting language.

_____ can demonstrate some of your past tone mistakes and
contrast them with new habits.

_____ can verify that you have completed most of the Get-
Connected Action Steps in this chapter.

Chapter 4

Nonverbal Communication

What You Don't Say Matters

In fifth grade, I learned about the 38th parallel—the heavily guarded line in the sand that separates North and South Korea. But I never expected to see a scale model of that boundary in my son's Language Arts class. Behind the barbed wire and sandbags (which only remotely resemble a desk), Ms. Bristle stood at attention, sporting a wide-eyed mechanical smile, and nodding curtly to parents as they entered.

Right away, we thought it odd that a teacher new to the district would appear so unwelcoming to her students' parents. It was doubly puzzling following on the heels of the welcome letter that came home with our son last week. That was a masterpiece! The letter outlined her impressive qualifications and her inspirational teaching philosophy. Her great objective, so she advertised, was to bond with each student and help her or him blossom personally and intellectually. Now, sitting in the teacher's presence, my wife and I looked at each other with the unspoken question, "What's wrong with this picture?"

She looked even more intimidating than she did unwelcoming (quite an accomplishment). She topped out at over six feet, and a severe black bun knot added another three inches. My wife leaned toward me and whispered, "Wow, I'll bet she doesn't have any discipline problems." I was too frightened to answer.

Ms. Bristle began a robotic presentation. There was nothing unnerving about her words. She said all the right things, albeit in a stiff and somewhat loud tone. But everything else she broadcast—wow! I did not move a muscle. With her feet planted firmly behind the 38th parallel, her arms locked across her chest like shields, she resolutely focused on something in the back of the room. Only her mouth moved.

As you can imagine, we left the Parent Open House full of questions, confusion, and foreboding. Our conversation in the car (the parts I can repeat) went something like this:

- "Is she human?"
- "What has she done with the woman who wrote that beautiful letter?"
- "Is she really a caring person, but just terrified of parents?"
- "Is she a heartless robot just spouting all the educational jargon she knows sounds good to parents?
- "Who IS she, really?"
- "How can our son spend a day here without being terrified?"

Just what this teacher wanted to convey to the parents, I am not sure; her intended message was not clear. Nevertheless, I learned some lessons that night in Room 34-B. I got a quick tutorial in the power of body language. Ms. Bristle (not her real name, of course) taught me to start "listening" to the unspoken communication in my classroom.

The Pitch 📢 ▬▬▬▬▬▬▬▬▬▬

You connect with students by showing acceptance with your body language. Facial expressions, posture, stance, movement, gestures, and many other nonverbal factors give strong messages of acceptance or non-acceptance. Words are important, but they don't tell the whole story. Decoding nonverbal signals is a fundamental skill within the art of learning to connect. Verbal and nonverbal signals, when taken all together, can be mixed and confusing—but I guarantee that in the classroom, your body language speaks more loudly than your voice—even if you yell.

To communicate well, one of your teacher jobs is to project the same welcoming, accepting messages nonverbally that you try to project verbally. Another job is to read those ever-present verbal signals from students. This chapter will train you as a nonverbal black belt! You'll tune in to the nonverbal world, examine your nonverbal patterns, and use body language to project authenticity and acceptance. Join the ideas in this chapter with what you learned in Chapter 3, and you'll have a powerful combination for connection. For this chapter on **communicating acceptance nonverbally**, your learning targets are:

Learning Targets

1. Identify your own nonverbal behaviors that show acceptance or nonacceptance.

2. Take new steps to "read" your students' nonverbal responses.

3. Practice nonverbal communication that shows acceptance and connection.

4. Project an integrated verbal and nonverbal message of connection.

Ramp Up Awareness

We're addicted to words. By "we," I mean teachers, though certainly this extends far beyond the schoolhouse! The advent of digital communication, I believe, has amplified this phenomenon. There are fewer face-to-face or voice-to-voice interactions. More and more, we communicate without the benefit of all those nonverbal signals that add richness and meaning to the communication.

When I stop to think about my own history with reading body language, I realize how natural this is! As a child, I could tell when Mom or Dad was angry before a word was spoken. Our dog understood several words, but it was when I grabbed the leash or picked up a ball that I saw the greatest response. And when I first tried to communicate with someone who did not speak my language—wow! It was amazing how much we understood each other. With lots of hand gestures and facial expressions, we had a conversation. So I'm delighted by this journey into reviving what I think comes naturally to humans and into reclaiming some of my lost nonverbal-communication skills.

I was well into the quest for better connections with students before the idea of body language crossed my radar screen. Of course, I knew about the concept of nonverbal communication, but it hadn't crossed my teacher-behavior radar screen. Then a few years ago, a few influences converged in a perfect storm, shook things up, and launched a rapid paradigm shift for me. One of them was the parents' night experience related at the opening of this story.

Another was quite a different story. Sitting in a doctor's waiting room, I listened to a podcast on my laptop. A segment on a book called *The Game* caught my interest. Journalist Neil Strauss, citing his own loneliness, decided to investigate whether there was a method that could help him to become more successful with women (a nice way to say "to pick up women"). He became a member of a group of guys who shared experience and knowledge. Since my passion is interpersonal relationships (and since I love to read an eclectic selection of books), this sounded too juicy to pass up. It was a funny book, and being happily married, I'll assure you that I was not out to become a pickup artist. But the author's passages on nonverbal communication inspired me to examine all kinds of interactions I have with friends, colleagues, students, and even strangers. I got fascinated with the whole realm of body language.

It was after that unusual readying foray that I began to gobble up articles on the subject. (I highly recommend *The Definitive Book of Body Language* by Barbara and Allan Pease.) Then I started to notice the power of nonverbal communication in presidential politics. During election seasons, I studied with fascination the nonverbal communication styles of candidates. I noticed things like stiff posture, relaxed shoulders, engaging smiles, lifted chins, arrogant smirks, warm hugs, wooden hugs, and shifty eyes. I thought about how such behaviors affected their messages or voter turnout.

More and more, I began to experiment with changes in my own nonverbal communication, particularly in my role as teacher and colleague. It has become crystal clear to me that this is an equal partner with words and actions in showing acceptance and connection. I've committed an entire chapter to this aspect of communication, because I have seen its power. I feel it's worth the space and your reading time for you to take stock of your own body language, pay attention to students' body language, and use what you learn to add dynamite results to your connections.

Author's Reflection

Okay, I have to stop and reminisce here. It may seem way off track and far, far away from classroom tales. But it's an important (and possibly the most memorable) part of my awareness about nonverbal communication.

The Ohio winter of 1977 was frigid! When you are 15, such winters can be magical. School was constantly cancelled, I socialized incessantly, and one of my closest friends was the first in our class to get his driver's license. Never mind that the roads were ice rinks— we became mobile! To celebrate his achievement, he, another buddy, and I decided to go on a triple date. Both of my friends had girlfriends, and I asked a girl whom I had not yet dated. She lived in a neighboring town, and I had been told that she liked me. I thought she was cute, so I rolled the dice, and she said "yes."

All six of us piled into the 1976 Cutlass Supreme. It was just my luck that my date sat in front and I sat in back. The radio was on

118

full blast and was full of static, and there was little conversation. So by the time we got to the theater, I had barely spoken to her. When we finally got to be side-by-side, she seemed happy to be there, but didn't say much. I couldn't decide whether she was shy or bored.

My brilliant friends selected the movie Rocky. I had never heard of Sylvester Stallone. In 1977, Sly was an impressive hunk! I was 140 pounds, at most. It was not a favorable comparison. When Sly popped on the screen, my young lady companion stared at him with her mouth open, as if in a trance. For two hours she watched this guy. I was feeling less and less confident about the date.

After the show, my driving friend (who had amazing courage and zero tact) said, "We have about an hour before the girls have to be home, so LET'S GO PARKING!" My date did not object.

Now, I have to explain the logistics of this. Remember, there were six of us in one car, and the outdoor temperature was 5 °F. While my friend was fearless, I was resourceful. I had a plan. I was wearing a wristwatch (kids used to wear wristwatches), and my idea was to have one couple leave the car for 10 minutes and take a walk. When they returned to the car (numb), they would knock on the window. The couple in the back would move to the front, the two in the front would go for a walk, and my shivering date and I would slide in the back. As I write this, I am amazed by how uninhibited (or nuts) we were. It's a beautiful memory.

"Kiss me you fool!"

Jim Sturtevant's sketch from memory.

My date warmed up in the cold night. We began talking. Back in the car, I was starting to feel more confident, and then it happened. I was working up the cour-

You've Gotta Connect

age to kiss her when I noticed that she looked strange. Her pupils were enormous. Granted, there was not a lot of light in the car, but this was not simple dilation. All I could see were these huge black pupils. Neil Strauss (author of the aforementioned book, The Game), *calls this "the doggy dinner bowl look." If you have a dog and you are not sure what that means, hold a treat in front of your dog and watch the eyes. I knew none of this in 1977, but instinctively I deduced that my date had it bad for me and indeed wanted me to kiss her. I was right.*

You ask, "Do you mean that you can tell if a girl wants you to kiss her just by looking at her pupils?" Oh yes! And how is this connected to accepting students? While kissing will definitely not be a part of your teaching strategies, you will discern much about someone's feelings or intent from looking at the eyes!

Learn to Read Signals

You can read a dozen books on nonverbal communication, and while that will be interesting, it does little good if you don't apply the research and information to yourself. I've taken many steps beyond reading. Reading is the fun part. The application can be fun, too. But the real growth includes some pain and hard work.

I say "pain" because I've had to learn some tough things about my nonverbal habits. I've had to bite the bullet and open myself to feedback from colleagues, students, and family members. As I've tuned in to students' body language, I've awakened to signals of things like frustration, boredom, disapproval, hurt, confusion, anger, or humiliation—all in response to my behavior. I say "hard work" because becoming aware of my own nonverbal communication takes work. Showing acceptance through body language takes persistence and practice. It also takes constant, relentless awareness. In addition, embracing and learning from students' nonverbal messages (without being defensive) takes humility. (That's work for some of us!)

For me, the body language checkup began with self-evaluation. Then it spread to more awareness of messages students transmit through their body language. I've developed a makeshift overview of body language ideas and questions in my quest to read body language and improve my own. As you read this, keep in mind that these questions should always be at the heart of your quest:

1. What messages does my body language project to students?

2. Are these the messages I want to project?

3. What does the body language of others reflect back to me about my words, presentation, or behavior in a given situation?

Make sure you tackle **Get-Connected Action Step 4.3** later in this chapter. Several exercises provide practice in reading a variety of nonverbal signals projected from head to toe.

A Caution: I'll focus on questions and comments about different areas of body language. It is critical to note that there is no one right way to interpret a particular nonverbal action or movement. Lowered eyes, tensed fists, or a step away can each mean different things. It all depends on the situation. Nonverbal clues are very important. Yet, to understand a person's response, nonverbal clues must be read in combination with other clues and information. Don't assume that lowered eyes always signal disinterest or that tensed fists always mean a person is ready to punch you. The point here is to pay attention to the body language and learn what it can tell you. It is more information for connecting.

Face

The face is usually the first part of the body noticed in an interchange. This is especially true if there are no other large or abrupt movements of the whole body, arms, or hands. Watch faces. Look

for the shape and activity of
the eyes. Watch movement and
position of eyebrows, forehead,
and mouth. (It's hard to watch
your own face, so you might
have to spend some time in
front of a mirror. Mostly, though
you'll have to trust others to
tell you what they see.)

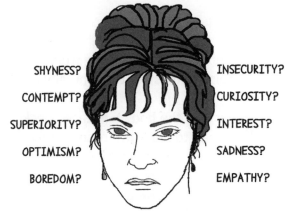

SHYNESS?
CONTEMPT?
SUPERIORITY?
OPTIMISM?
BOREDOM?

INSECURITY?
CURIOSITY?
INTEREST?
SADNESS?
EMPATHY?

Are eyes narrowed, relaxed, widened, or closed? Are they lowered or
looking directly at you? Are they focused on you, or are they focused
somewhere else? Are they staring? Are they glaring? Are they laughing
or twinkling? Are they teary? Are they blinking? Are they shifting? Are
eyebrows raised, pulled together, or dropped?

Is the forehead scrunched or relaxed? Is the mouth or jaw dropped
in a scowl? Are lips narrow and tense? Are they pressed together?
Are they twitching in a slight smile? Is there a broad, carefree smile?
Are the lips in a sneer? Are the lips smiling without any other signs in
the face of a genuine smile? (When you smile and mean it, your eyes
narrow.)

What's the position of the head? Is it tipped down? Is it tilted to the
side? Is it held high with chin out? Is the head laid down on the desk?
Is the head tilted forward so that hair purposely hides the face? Are
hands covering all or part of the face? Is the face hidden behind a
notebook, book, hoodie, or other object?

Ask
Yourself:

Do I use
fake smiles?

Lowered eyes might signal submission, insecurity, or
fear. They could signal hesitation or thoughtfulness. They
might signal shyness, shame, coyness, or embarrassment.
When someone's eyes narrow and the eyebrows drop, she
might be concentrating. Or she might be challenging you.
Or she could be angry. Widened eyes, especially when

accompanied by raised eyebrows, may show surprise, shock, great interest, or amusement. I know someone whose eyes widen when he feels afraid or threatened. Blinking, shifting eyes might signal boredom, nervousness, disagreement, or an urge to escape. Or, the person might have a speck of dust in his eye. Or she might be fighting to stay awake!

A stare can mean many things. It might signal unabashed curiosity. It could signal an effort to hold in emotion. It could be a challenge. A distinct glare seems more clearly to signal a challenge, anger, or disapproval. (Try not to get into staring contests, by the way. If this happens, break the stare-fest with a smile.)

A lowered head may be a sign of shyness, withdrawal, self-doubt, or shame. Or, it may be a sign that the person is thinking seriously about something. A tilted head could show challenge or confusion.

Arms & Hands

Arms and hands are incredibly expressive extensions. I get a kick out of watching hand talkers like my wife Penny. Even when she is on the phone, she will make arm and hand motions as if the listener could see her. I once watched her in the school office giving standardized test instructions to the sophomore class over the PA. None of them could see her, but when she instructed them to turn the page, she of course turned an imaginary page in a dramatic fashion. It caused a lot of laughter among those present because we've all been long amused by her proclivity for hand and arm flinging.

"You might be choking or crying, but I have emails to send."

Watch the hands and arms. Are the arms flinging or hands waving? Are hands pulling at hair or shoved in pockets? Are the hands and arms used to demonstrate or punctuate the person's spoken language? Is he chewing on his nails or fingers? Is she clenching her fists, cracking her knuckles, or wringing her hands? Are the hands shaking or fidgeting? Are they relaxed? Are the palms turned out? Are arms crossed firmly across the chest? Are they held stiffly at the sides? Are they relaxed? Are arms or hands hanging onto someone else (or annoying someone else)?

Hands can give signals of many feelings or responses, among them nervousness, welcome, passion, acceptance, excitement, tension, or protection, or defense. Waving hands can show that the person is eager or excited. Or they can betray a person's need to push something away or protect herself. Hand fidgeting or wringing can show tension, impatience, worry, anger, or boredom. Hands across the chest can mean, "Leave me alone," "I'm self-conscious," or "I'm tough; don't mess with me." If the arms are laid casually and loosely across the chest, this could signal a relaxed, easy state.

Legs & Feet

In economics, we study "leading economic indicators." The government measures these statistics on a monthly basis. Here's an example: Applications for building permits are tallied. An increase in applications points to economic growth in the near future. Successful economists read this signal, and a whole slate of others, to accurately predict what will happen in the future. In body language, the feet are the "leading intention indicators" of where the body will to go. Pay attention to feet—their stance and their movement.

Are the feet pointed toward you and standing still? Are they turned away from you? Does the person step toward you? Does he rock back and forth or from side to side while talking? Does the person take steps backwards while interacting with you? Are the feet pacing? Is the stance of the legs and feet somewhat open and relaxed? When seated, does she cross her legs? Are feet held tightly together? Is he shaking his leg or wiggling a foot?

A tremor is felt throughout Jackson Middle School.

If someone with whom you are talking does not turn the feet toward you, there's a good chance that the visit will be short. Maybe she is in a hurry, or maybe he does not want this encounter to last long—whether he has any other place to be or not. Maybe she's keeping a distance or wants to be ready to leave at any moment. If the feet are turned toward you, the person is probably more focused and in no hurry to leave. If the feet are planted firmly, this may signal stubbornness, resolution, or aggression. Or it may just signal eagerness to be there! A shaking foot or leg might signal anxiety or boredom (or too much coffee).

Posture

Posture is one of the easiest aspects of body language to read. Most likely, it is because posture (or stance) contains so many signals that work together to show someone's state of mind, attitude, or health. (By posture, I mean the stance—or the overall way the body is carried or positioned.) Most teachers can tell when a student (or colleague) is having a bad day just from looking at the posture. Try to recall a depressed or frightened student who had awesome posture. Any luck? This is not to say that posture can't project false signals; but in general, posture broadcasts the real story.

As a part of knowing and accepting students, pay attention to the whole body language. Is he holding his head high and moving with confidence (but not cockiness)? Does she move with stiffness and caution? Does he lean forward to engage someone else, or lean away, or turn sideways? Does she wrap her arms around her protectively?

You've Gotta Connect

Ask Yourself:

*Do I show
disapproval
or disinterest
with nonverbal
signals?*

Since posture involves movement or placement of arms, hands, legs, feet, trunk, and the head, many of the other signals mentioned in previous sections come into play. Look for the big picture that will convey such impressions as comfort, fear, openness, energy, weariness, discomfort, reluctance, suspicion, trust, despair, hopelessness, or hope.

When it comes to the teacher's posture, know that you, too, project your state of mind loudly with the way you carry your body. Your posture can help you connect with students or contribute to disconnection. Your stance in the presence of students can give out messages of acceptance or nonacceptance. Your posture can help you teach a lesson effectively or get in the way of successful teaching. Here are a few words of wisdom for using posture to show students you accept them and want to connect:

- In general, use your posture to be warm and inviting. Think "openness." Use your body to let students know you welcome them and want to engage them.

- Face a student fully and not halfway. Step toward the student, lean slightly in, keeping arms out.

- Never use your posture or stance to intimidate or threaten a student. Avoid puffing up your chest or lowering your chin as if you're getting ready for a head-butt.

- Use your body to show confidence and comfort. It's reassuring to students to know you are comfortably in charge. Keep your shoulders and arms relaxed. Keep your head back with chin up.

- Slow down. Unless you are on one of your *life or death* missions (teachers do have these once in a while), stop darting from point A to point B. The frenzied movement speaks this message to students: "I'm way too busy to pay attention to you." Cut back the pace. Take longer strides. Keep your arms relaxed and swinging effortlessly as you walk. Try it. It feels great.

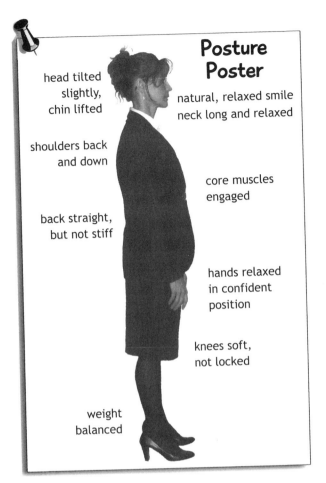

Posture Poster

head tilted slightly, chin lifted

natural, relaxed smile
neck long and relaxed

shoulders back and down

core muscles engaged

back straight, but not stiff

hands relaxed in confident position

knees soft, not locked

weight balanced

My lovely wife Penny has fantastic posture. This is her typical stance. I've used her example to set my own goals for posture that conveys messages I want to project. She's a virtual poster child for the confident, warm, reassuring teacher. (Actually, she's the principal.) She is warm and inviting, but at the same time, she's no pushover.

Whether you are standing still, sitting, or moving, practice good posture. Once your body adjusts, better posture feels wonderful. Its effects are akin to the effects of meditation. When I am walking down the hall lost in life's drama, I stop, lengthen my neck, and drop my shoulders back and down. Ahhh, that feels better!

Join Forces

This is the most important section of the chapter. "Well, if that's so," you're probably asking, "then why are you just now getting around to it?"

I wanted to give you the easiest tasks first—examining the way you use body language and gauging its effects on connection with students. I saved this part for later because it's scarier. But now you're ready. So here it is: **Ask your students to teach you about your body language.** In the last chapter, I insisted that your students know which of your verbal habits show acceptance and which do not. You cannot see your own body language. Only the other persons see that. And your students see more of it than anyone else at school and possibly more than anyone outside of school. (You can be sure they can mimic you perfectly.) So put pride aside and take the leap to enlist your students in this whole venture of improving nonverbal communication.

When a teacher sits while teaching, I feel more like he is with me and is my friend.

- Make nonverbal communication part of your classroom dialogue. It's fascinating stuff. Your students will be intrigued. Share the information and ideas in the previous section, "Learn to Read Signals." Ask students to pay more attention to all these aspects of your behavior and their own. As they reflect back to you, they'll learn some things about themselves. Set procedures whereby this kind of discussion is held respectfully.

- Ask students such questions as
  How do I show approval (nonverbally)? How do I show disapproval?
  Do I ever give off signals that I'm withdrawing from you? What do you see?
  I have a habit of crossing my hands behind my head. What message does that project to you?
  What nonverbal patterns of mine give you confusing signals?

- Design a survey to get more information from students. **Get-Connect-ed Action Step 4.1,** later in this chapter, will help you enlists students to increase your body language patterns.

- Watch students' nonverbal responses to you. Follow up to find out what they mean. For example, ask questions such as
  Okay, what did I just do that led to the rolling eyes?
  I see that about 15 of you just sunk lower into your seats. What did I do?

See **Get-Connected Action Step 4.2** found later in this chapter. It guides you through an exercise in noticing and reflecting on nonverbal messages sent by your students.

▪ Practice body language that communicates welcoming, accepting messages. Ask students how you're doing with your attempts. See **Get-Connected Action Step 4.5** later in this chapter. It guides you in a review of what you've learned about your body language. When you take the action step, you'll also set goals for projecting more positive messages.

Before you move into the action steps with their concentrated practice, consider these last bits of advice:

1. **Join forces with colleagues, too.** Ask them to feed back what they notice about your nonverbal communication with them and with your students. Seek their observations about how your body language changes when you are threatened or uncomfortable. Ask them to point out your nonverbal habits that obviously affirm and connect with students.

2. **Nonverbal communication is a two-way street.** If you get too focused on what you are seeing, you will forget what you are broadcasting. Your nonverbal signals and your students' play off each other. You can learn from each other.

3. **Verbal communication and nonverbal communication are partners.** Know that they support or compete with one another. Be aware of the ways they work together to give the message you want to give or do not intend to give.

4. **Don't fixate on one signal.** I once taught a student with an intense stare. She would lower her eyebrows and stare at me. I thought she was angry or upset a lot. It confused me because she was such a nice, cooperative kid. The rest of her body language was open and friendly.

You've Gotta Connect

The boys were completely intimidated by her. So was I. Eventually, I learned that her stare was just what happened when she concentrated. I think she has a future as a negotiator.

5. **Have fun with nonverbal communication.** Once you become aware of this under-the-radar language, interactions get really interesting. After a conversation, you can analyze the signals sent and received. The more you practice, the better you'll get at this skill.

6. **In every interaction, you're building rapport** (even if your goal is to give out such information as: "Today we're beginning Unit Four.") To succeed, be aware of all the signals you transmit. In teacher-student communication, the dominance-submission dynamic is a factor. There are times when you have to be assertive and times, when a student is defensive, that you need to reduce the student's anxiety. It's so helpful to be able to read the situation and adapt on the fly. Read the students' signals and adjust yours. Have fun with **Get-Connected Action Step 4.4.** You'll mirror someone else's body language.

Listen to Students

It's so connecting when the teacher gives a simple high five or knuckle bump!

Author's Reflection

A few years ago I made the startling discovery that forced some adjustment. I realized that I was not making eye contact with my students. During lessons, I focused on about three inanimate objects around the room. Apparently I was uncomfortable! My work on nonverbal communication brought this to my awareness. Eye contact is an intensely intimate act, and it's understandable that people might look away. However, I knew there was no way to create a bond with students unless I looked at them.

I have worked hard to break this habit. Here's a progress report: The desks in my class are set in a U shape. I walk around in the open space in the front and pontificate. I made a plan to look at a student's face on one side, make my point, smile and nod, then repeat the process for the other sides. Next, I return to the first side, and choose a different student. By the time I'm done with my spiel, I have made eye contact with most students.

Granted, there is nothing revolutionary about this method, but I have added a little twist. Now, I say the student's name when I make eye contact: "And Marcus, do you know what those crazy Romans did?" Marcus often remains silent, so I forge ahead, "I'll tell you what they did! They ...." Marcus feels he contributed.

This practice has made eye contact easy. I no longer have to stare down the globe, the clock, or the upper right windowpane.

When I first developed this interest in body language, I thought, "How useful for an educator." I was right. What I didn't anticipate was that my newfound skill became a great barometer for measuring the effectiveness of all my interactions, even those with my wife! (But now, that's another book!)

If you can be honest with yourself about your patterns; if you can be open to what others reflect back to you; if you can resist feeling silly or defensive—you'll find you can change body language with some simple adjustments. Yes! Improvement **is** within your grasp. Keep moving toward improvement with the action steps that follow.

Then, don't neglect to finish the chapter by summarizing what you learned in the chapter. See the **Learning Targets Checklist** on the final page of Chapter 4.

Get-Connected! Action Steps

Action Step 4.1 What Do I Broadcast?

Here's a chance to learn about the nonverbal messages you project to your students. Now that you've read the ideas and examples in this chapter, you should have a read on how you show students you accept them (or how you show something else).

1. Begin with a discussion about teacher body language. Ask students to act out or mimic some generic teacher behavior that shows acceptance or nonacceptance of students. Tell them not to name any teachers. Have fun with this, but let them know that you are seriously interested in examining your own nonverbal communications with students.

2. For each behavior they show, ask them to describe the signal or message they believe the behavior projects.

3. Talk about some of the body language ideas from this chapter. Ask them to give general examples of such behaviors from their peers, teachers, or themselves (eyes, faces, hands and arms, legs and feet, posture). Talk about the idea that people often don't recognize these behaviors in themselves.

4. Use the form **The Teacher's Nonverbal Signals** on page 138. Project this where all students can see it or give each student a copy. Ask them to list up to 10 of **your** nonverbal behaviors that are familiar to them. (You might give this at the beginning of class or at the beginning of a week and ask them to watch, collecting these over a period of time.) Encourage them to watch for behaviors that signal acceptance or nonacceptance of one or more individuals.

5. For each behavior listed, the student should write a comment about what message that behavior projects. Students do not have to write their names.

6. Here's the part where you need to get brave. Ask students to share their examples of things you do that give negative or positive messages. This may happen within a discussion or by collecting their papers. Be sure you make it safe for students to be honest. Show genuine interest in building positive nonverbal communication skills. Mimic (with exaggeration) your own behaviors that students list. Ask them, "Is this what you are talking about?"

7. Learn from this! For example, ask: "How would I need to change my body language to change that message?" or "What would be a better alternative for my nonverbal response?"

8. When students identify behaviors or suggestions that ring true and make sense to you, set some goals for improvement. Share the goals with students. Then follow up. Ask students later, "How am I doing at ____?" This shows a true openness to improvement.

Action Step 4.2 What Do Students Broadcast?

Now it's time to take a close look at students' body language. Start paying attention to those nonverbal behaviors that flash before you many times a day!

1. Every day for a week, notice gestures, expressions, or other nonverbal clues you pick up from students' responses to you. This can be from an individual or a group of students.

2. Use the **Students' Nonverbal Signals** form on page 139. Choose 10 of the nonverbal clues and list them on the form.

3. For each clue, draw (and write) a conclusion about what feeling or message this communicates.

4. Find a time to share your reflections with your students. Ask them if you are reading them right.

5. Take some time to discuss alternatives to body language that gives non-accepting or disconnecting messages.

6. You might add a step where students set personal goals for their own nonverbal communication skills. They'd probably love to do this exercise about each other. If you try this, handle it carefully so no one is making fun of, cruelly mimicking, or criticizing another student.

Action Step 4.3 Without a Word

Take an inventory of some nonverbal messages. The next four pages show examples of nonverbal expressions, stances, postures, and gestures. This exercise will give practice in "reading" and responding to these.

1. Start with page 140, **Nonverbal Inventory: The Face.** Examine each picture. Write a response to each one, noting what message or feeling you feel is conveyed. (If you were a student receiving this "look" during an interaction with this person, what message would you believe was being sent your way?)

2. Go on to pages 141-143, **Nonverbal Inventory: The Arms & Hands, Nonverbal Inventory: The Legs & Feet,** and **Nonverbal Inventory:**

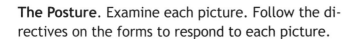

The Posture. Examine each picture. Follow the directives on the forms to respond to each picture.

3. Discuss these with colleagues or students. There are no right or wrong answers. What is important is the impression you get from someone else's body language. Even more important is your self-reflection about the kinds of impressions you give through nonverbal means. Talk about what you learned from this exercise.

Action Step 4.4 Mirror Movements

Once you and your students become more accomplished at reading body language and projecting nonverbal signals accurately, try this fun activity.

1. Choose a person with whom you want to form a stronger bond. You might start with one of your colleagues and try it later with a student. Do this exercise in a situation where you involved in some sort of interaction with that person.

2. Without letting the person know, mirror her or his body language. Do this subtly—no exaggeration. The biggest challenge is to keep a straight face. The most interesting aspect is seeing how long it takes the other person to notice.

3. Watch what happens as you do this. Even though the other person is not aware of what you are doing, it is amazing how receptive he or she becomes when his or her signals are duplicated.

You've Gotta Connect

Action Step 4.5   On a Mission

If you've spent five minutes working in a school district, you have been exposed to mission statements. This is all the rage in schools, so when in Rome, let's do as the Romans do. Administrators love to craft mission statements, and they expect teachers to embrace them enthusiastically. This mission statement, however, is yours.

1. Review all that you have learned about nonverbal communication from this chapter, from your discussions with students or colleagues, and from the actions steps. Think about the patterns you have identified in your own body language.

2. Jot down a list of your body language patterns that you have identified (or your students have identified for you). Write them in two columns: behaviors that signal acceptance or connection and behaviors that signal nonacceptance or disconnection. (See the example on facing page.)

3. From the first list, select five or six nonverbal behaviors you would like to use more often to connect to students. From the second list, select five or six behaviors you would like to eliminate from your body language. Use the **Body-Language Reflection** form on page 144 to record your choices.

4. Use the selected behaviors as raw material for a general, summarizing mission statement. Write a brief paragraph that states your plan of attack or mission you will pursue related to body language.

5. Write today's date at the bottom of the page. Write another date that is four to six weeks from now. On that date, review this list and mission statement to check on your progress. You can ask your students to help. Ask them to reflect on how well you are keeping to your mission.

My Body-Language Profile

Behaviors and actions that signal acceptance or connect me to students:	Behaviors or actions that signal nonacceptance or disconnect me from students:
• *welcoming at classroom door with friendly smile and stance*	• *waving arms and shaking head*
• *nodding kindly as I listen*	• *rolling eyes when a student is talking*
• *giving high fives*	• *smirking*
• *making smiling eye contact with each student each day*	• *backing away*
• *sitting on edge of desk closer to students*	• *standing with feet apart and arms crossed over chest*
• *smiling at appropriate jokes, even if slightly weird*	• *retreating behind desk*
• *laughing with students at myself*	• *glaring*
• *keeping a neutral face and stance when a conflict arises*	• *planting feet, hands on hips with scowl*
• *staying calm when challenged*	• *stomping toward a troublemaker*
	• *giving a grin or chuckle to some students when another student is showing lack of preparation*
	• *taking deep, disgusted sighs*

THE TEACHER'S NONVERBAL SIGNALS

What the Teacher Does   **The Message This Projects**

1. ———————————————➤ ————————————————

————————————————————— ————————————————

2. ———————————————➤ ————————————————

————————————————————— ————————————————

3. ———————————————➤ ————————————————

————————————————————— ————————————————

4. ———————————————➤ ————————————————

————————————————————— ————————————————

5. ———————————————➤ ————————————————

————————————————————— ————————————————

6. ———————————————➤ ————————————————

————————————————————— ————————————————

7. ———————————————➤ ————————————————

————————————————————— ————————————————

8. ———————————————➤ ————————————————

————————————————————— ————————————————

9. ———————————————➤ ————————————————

————————————————————— ————————————————

10. ———————————————➤ ————————————————

————————————————————— ————————————————

STUDENTS' NONVERBAL SIGNALS

What They Do

The Message I Get

1. ———————————————————▶

2. ———————————————————▶

3. ———————————————————▶

4. ———————————————————▶

5. ———————————————————▶

6. ———————————————————▶

7. ———————————————————▶

8. ———————————————————▶

9. ———————————————————▶

10. ———————————————————▶

You've Gotta Connect

Nonverbal Inventory: The Face

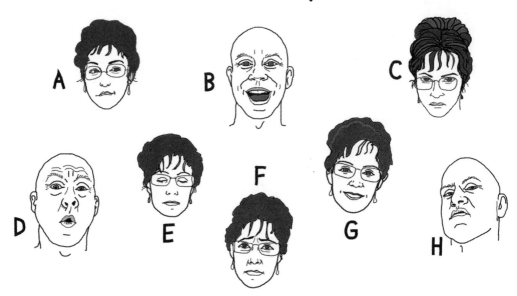

What message do you believe this look broadcasts?

A _____

B _____

C _____

D _____

E _____

F _____

G _____

H _____

Which of these "looks" do you use regularly?

Nonverbal Inventory: **The Arms & Hands**

What message is communicated by the position or
use of the arms and hands?

A _____

B _____

C _____

D _____

E _____

Which of these gestures do you use regularly?

You've Gotta Connect

Nonverbal Inventory: The Legs & Feet

A B C D E

What message is broadcast by the position or use of the feet and legs?

A _____

B _____

C _____

D _____

E _____

Which of these gestures do you use regularly?

You've Gotta Connect   **142**

Nonverbal Inventory: **The Posture**

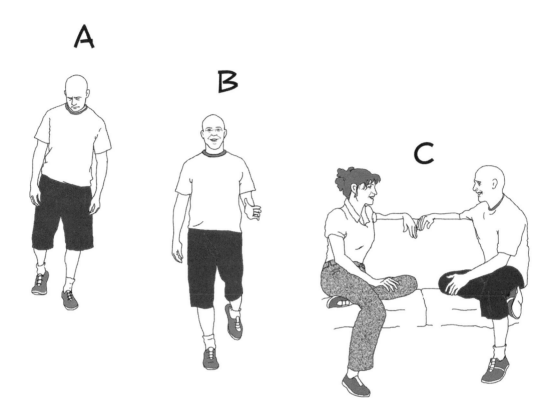

A

B

C

What message is projected by the body position, posture, or stance in each picture?

A _____

B _____

C _____

Which of these gestures do you use regularly?

You've Gotta Connect

Reproduce this page at 120% for 8½ x 11 size.

Body-Language Reflection

Behaviors and actions that signal acceptance or connect me to students:

Behaviors or actions that signal nonacceptance or disconnect me from students:

My Body-Language Mission Statement

_____
_____
_____
_____
_____
_____
_____
_____
_____
_____
_____

✔ Learning Targets Checklist

To summarize what you have learned in this chapter,
check ✓ if you . . .

_____ can dentify several examples of students' body language
that you have learned to "read."

_____ can describe, in general, how learning about body
language has affected life in your classroom.

_____ can restate several examples of feedback students
have given regarding your positive and negative body
language.

_____ are able to name at least five nonverbal behaviors that
you have learned show acceptance to students, and thus
you will keep using the behaviors.

_____ are able to name at least five nonverbal behaviors
that you have re-examined and replaced with more
connecting behaviors.

_____ can verify that you have completed most of the Get-
Connected Action Steps in this chapter.

You've Gotta Connect

Chapter 5

Safety

They've Gotta Know You Have Their Backs

I've started asking students wherever I go to share their actual experiences of teachers who show acceptance (or lack of it) and connection (or lack or it). This is risky business, because I usually hear some uncomfortable things about myself. It's also risky because, though I ask students not to name any other teachers, I hear still hear things that I must hold carefully, honoring the confidentiality. Here, I share some comments that relate specifically to safety they feel as learners. The voices belong to students ranging from students grades 8 through 12.

My math teacher told me I would be one of the most successful people because of how hard I work. That was the first time I have heard that from a teacher. He is the only teacher who has directly addressed my efforts.

Teachers show disconnection when they do not take the time to help students who are failing.

Here is something a teacher said that made me feel she cared about me: "This lesson is going to make you better."

When teachers care enough to make their subject matter interesting, they show connection to students.

One teacher finally took notice of my potential and skill in math after a few weeks in his pre-algebra class; so then he let me sit in an Algebra class. Then he moved me up to the next level class. It meant so much to me that he actually made an effort to help me challenge myself academically.

I feel accepted by teachers who help me with schoolwork and make learning fun.

One of the most disconnecting acts a teacher can do is to not explain things correctly.

A teacher can show acceptance to students by using the modern technology that we are used to and involving it in our education.

A teacher told one of my class groups that we students "could not think logically" due to our inexperience. I was appalled. Maybe my lack of experience does make my brain less mature. But to tell me that I cannot process thought in a logical manner is cruel. I am smart! I am thoughtful! I am capable of thinking for myself!

By taking time during lunch or after school to help me understand a topic, a teacher connects to me.

A teacher can instantly turn a student against learning when they have an attitude that makes the students gloomy.

I feel connection from a teacher who makes it possible to do assignments online.

Here's the most disconnecting thing a teacher has ever done to me: I got up the courage to approach my second grade teacher to tell her that the class work was too easy for me. She said she would not give me any challenging work because she wanted to keep the whole class on the same level.

This act of acceptance has stayed with me for years: I was not even in this teacher's class, but I was struggling with a project and she stayed after school to help me get it done.

When I listen to the voices of students, I always learn something. What stunned me about these statements was this: How powerful are their experiences of connection or disconnection with teachers! How long-lasting are the messages of acceptance or nonacceptance!

Let the students' words set the stage for this chapter about what it's like to be a student in your classroom and how you can connect in ways that help students believe in themselves as learners.

The Pitch

You connect with students by making your classroom a safe, comfortable place to learn. Students can't learn when they feel anxious, unsupported, fearful, misunderstood, or confused. Teacher-student connections have little chance to thrive in an atmosphere where students are uncertain about what will happen.

Students feel safe when they know that they will be welcomed, affirmed, supported, and respected; when they know they will be protected from intimidation or humiliation; when they know what to expect; when they know the rules and procedures; when they know the consequences for inappropriate behavior; when they know that the teacher is their advocate; and when they know they have a good chance to succeed academically.

As you can see, safety in the classroom includes physical safety, emotional safety, and academic safety. You can also see that this topic includes a host of components—teacher presence and attitude, peer relationships and behaviors, teaching skill and strategies, classroom rules and procedures, and academic expectations.

In this chapter, I challenge you to evaluate the safety of your classroom. I'll ask you to take concrete steps to show students that you have their backs. I'll recommend that you let them know you intend to help them enjoy themselves, and at the same time, learn well in your class. You can start building strong connections on the first day of class. Right away, students will relax, enjoy, and start believing they can trust you.

For this chapter on **safety**, these are the target areas for your learning:

Learning Targets

1. Do a safety inspection in your classroom and plan to improve where necessary.

2. Take stock of what it's like to be in your class.

3. Review your plans for how you will introduce students to you, to what will happen in your class, and to what they will learn.

4. Clearly communicate your behavioral and academic expectations to students.

5. Identify the consequences in your classroom for inappropriate behavior and examine your level of follow-through.

6. Grow as a warm demander.

Check Your Mindset

To embark on a successful journey that first day of the year or the semester, we teachers have some grand tasks to master. We must

- roll out the red carpet for our students

- captivate our audience

- anticipate some "day one" dynamics

- be ready to set the tone for the entire year

- introduce students to what they will learn

- explain all the procedures and expectations

Ask Yourself:

What is it like to be in my class?

But that's getting ahead of the game, because there's something to do before those plans are set or executed. We must embrace the privilege that is ours—the privilege to teach! As you plan for the upcoming year, semester, or courses, take time to pause and reflect on these: Consider

- what an awesome gift it is to be a partner in students' learning

- what you can learn from hanging out with these young people and watching them grow

- the impact you **could** (and **do**) have on these young people

- how rapidly your students are evolving and how receptive they are to many stimuli

- the fact that your students are nervous too—about dozens of factors and issues. (We sometimes forget this. Most of them have spent a lot of time getting ready to look good for peers they haven't seen all summer. They're anxious about social relationships and acceptance. All their classes are new to them. Their teacher or teachers are new. They are not sure what to expect. They may have cocky exteriors—especially those adolescents, but in reality they are not that far removed from the scared little kid Mama put on the bus the first day of kindergarten.)

Are you properly humbled? I hope so! Don't start school without a brainscan of your mindset! Tap into your love of teaching. Let the excitement (and nervousness) of meeting a new group of awesome students flow through you. Approach the year with commitment to make things work well for **all** your students. Then, with that sense of awe and privilege, get prepared! Don't just sail along on last year's plans.

Do a Safety Inspection

You cannot have connection without safety; it's that simple. Before you embark on a new school year or semester, focus on the aspects of safety (or lack of safety) that play a role in your classroom. Examine the procedures and approaches you have followed in the past (or neglected to follow). Start by asking yourself these kinds of questions:

- *Do undercurrents of threat flow around the classroom?*
- *Are any students subtly bullied?*
- *Are there any messages that some students are smarter than others?*
- *Are any students humiliated?*
- *Do I poke fun at students?*
- *Are any students ignored (by me or other students)?*
- *Do students make fun of other students?*
- *Is there any name-calling?*
- *Do I respond to any students with disregard or irritation?*
- *Is the seating arrangement safe for everyone?*
- *Do I show that I believe in each individual as a student?*
- *Do all students know they can get help with class work?*
- *Do I allow words or acts of disrespect to students?*
- *Do I follow procedures that are set out?*
- *Do I treat all students with equal regard?*
- *Do I apply rules and consequences the same to all students?*
- *Would any students doubt that I am their advocate?*
- *Do students leave class confused about concepts I taught?*
- *Do students feel confused about behavioral or academic expectations?*
- *Do any students get the message that they are failures?*

Ask Yourself:

Does any student in my class spend any time being afraid?

You've Gotta Connect

As you start to focus on safety, you'll be surprised at how many more questions pop up. The issue of safety pervades all aspects of classroom life. At the end of this chapter, you'll have a chance to do an official safety check of your classroom. See **Get-Connected Action Step 5.1** on page 172. Once you identify some areas of weakness, use the information in this chapter to help with your plans for upgrading the safety level in your classroom. Please don't do the safety check and shove it in a drawer. Make an improvement plan. Revisit that plan several times over the school year.

Plan That First Impression ▬▬▬▬

Life is crammed full of first impression scenarios . . .
- *a first date*
- *a job interview*
- *your first kiss*
- *meeting your fiancée's parents*
- *the first day of football practice*
- *the first day on a new job*
- *your first day reading lines in play practice*
- *the first time the professor calls on you*
- *an opening statement as a lawyer in mock trial*
- *your first weeks as a new parent (or first 18 years!!)*
- *the first time your significant other sees you in a bathing suit (Yikes!)*

Reminisce about some "firsts" in your life. That old adage is so true: "You never have a second chance to make a first impression." As a teacher, you do get a chance to make a first impression again and again each new year with each new class. Day One of the school year or semester is **opening night.** You want a performance that will leave the critics, your students, gushing!

Roll out the red carpet for students. The message of connection, disconnection, acceptance, or nonacceptance begins even before they walk in the door. Humans have an intuitive sense of whether they are welcome. Start by being there—outside the classroom door—greeting the students with warmth and enthusiasm. Obviously, this must be done the first day. The challenge is to do it every day. Students need to feel an open and genuine invitation each day to enter your little Cathedral of Learning.*

Be prepared; have all of your plans and supplies in place. If you are stationed at your door welcoming students with your warmest smile, this means that you can't be rushing around getting last-minute tasks done. These two things do not go together. You might protest: "I have four minutes between classes! That is the only time that I have to make additional copies, contact colleagues, go to the office, collate make-up work, or for the love of Pete, go to the bathroom!"

Realistically, you will have to do some things just before class now and then. However, make it a practice to have everything ready, or for the moment on hold, when students arrive. They need to know that your absolute first priority is to welcome them!

What will students feel about you and your class by the time the class begins? Will the first impression allow them to relax a bit and start to think this could be a good year? Will they be more terrified than they were before they arrived? You have plenty of work to do in the first days to get off to a good start. You will have taken a giant step forward if the first impression is agreeable. Use the ideas and suggestions in the remaining sections of this chapter to help you make that first impression the right one.

---

* I grew up an hour and a half west of Pittsburgh, Pennsylvania. The University of Pittsburgh has a beautiful gothic skyscraper that dominates the campus. It's named the Cathedral of Learning and is a structure that fascinates me! I have always referred to my classroom as the Cathedral of Learning in honor of the Pitt Panthers.

You've Gotta Connect

Set the Tone

First impressions continue inside the room. You begin to set the tone before the bell rings. You broaden your welcome once kids are in their seats. Hopefully you have asked yourself the question, "What do I want students to know when they walk out the door at the end of the first day or class?"

This first day is the time to make the main statements about what it will be like to be in your class. (These won't all be made with words.) Choose the statements carefully. If you believe that connection is one of your first commitments to students, plan your opening class in that context.

To set the tone around connection and safety, I suggest that you don't let students out of your room on that first day before you

- tell them that you feel it is an honor to be their teacher.
- communicate that relationships are going to be top priority.
- let them know you are kind, friendly, and in charge.
- show that you are confident and prepared.
- inform them of the purposes and learning goals of the class.
- say that you see it as your job to help them succeed in this class.
- assure them that you'll make all procedures and expectations clear.
- make an obvious attempt to learn their names.
- show energy and passion for the class and your job.
- make it clear that respect and kindness are central themes in your class.
- demonstrate your respect for them as individuals and as a group.
- communicate that this will be a place where learning is taken seriously.
- communicate that you will work hard to make learning interesting and relevant.

- assure them that you are their advocate.

- give them signals that you are human and approachable.

- show that you are interested in their ideas, opinions, and feedback.

SAFETY ZONE

No Hard Hats Needed

Grade 8 English

Mrs. Ruiz

As a part of communicating these messages,

1. **Do a learning activity.** You've said that you take learning seriously. Make sure a dynamic learning experience is part of the first day. It can be short if time is limited, but make sure they learn something new and fascinating.

2. **Get students out of their seats.** You've promised to make learning interesting. So don't be boring. Get them moving and interacting.

3. **Give them a voice.** Ask for feedback, opinions, or observations from them. You've told them that you are interested in their ideas. Show this on the first day. Plan something that lets student voices be heard. This might be the personal survey from Chapter 3, Get-Connected Action Step 3.2 or the survey of teacher coolness from Chapter 3, Get-Connected Action Step 3.1. Or you might ask them to share opinions in answer to one question such as: "What is the best learning experience you have had or would like to have?" or "What's one thing that makes you feel comfortable in a classroom or with a teacher?"

   Listen to Students

4. **Tell them something about yourself.** Include some humor. This is an avenue for showing them how you are human and approachable.

   Teachers connect to students by making their subject matter interesting.

You've Gotta Connect

As you plan for setting a tone of connection in your classroom, try **Get-Connected Action Step 5.2** later in this chapter. It includes an interesting self-interview to help you consider about what you want students to know and think when they leave your classroom after Day One.

But what about the rules, you ask? Isn't that the most important thing to do on the first day? I have not excluded that. However, all of the above is more important than the rules—and is actually a foundation for any classroom expectations.

Clarify Expectations

"This first day is the time to make the main statements about what it will be like to be in your class." This is a direct quote from earlier in the chapter. As you've made your initial, welcoming impression and taken steps to set the tone for the year, you have already started on the path of letting them know what it will be like to be in your class. Now we come to some big topics—two things that must be a part of your first day or first few days.

1. Students must get a feel for what they can expect to learn in your class.

2. Students must be told what will be expected of them and what they can expect of you.

Expectations in a classroom—this is a broad topic! It includes behavioral, academic, and procedural stuff. Students have a right to know what is expected of them in all these areas. Your chances of having a smooth (or relatively smooth) school year are greatest if you communicate expectations clearly and right away. Tackling these topics gives you a golden opportunity to bond with your students, allay their fears, build their academic confidence, deter potential problems, and leave them feeling safe. At the same time, you can make great first impression and everyone can have some fun.

When you plan for your first days of school or the semester, make absolutely sure you have a way to give clear and direct information about

- what the class is about

- what topics you'll be covering

- the kinds of learning activities they'll be doing

- how they can participate

- all the procedures for doing work (including homework) and turning it in

- how their work and participation will be evaluated

- what it means to be a serious student who does his or her best

- how they can get help from you

- how you will treat them

- how they will treat each other and you

- the basic behavioral understandings

- the consequences for inappropriate behavior

- all the procedures for getting things done in the classroom

Teachers connect to students by making their subject matter interesting.

I have seen many teachers make a big mistake when they talk to students about expectations. They make this all long and complicated. They compound the mistake by presenting it in a stifling fashion. Often they are totally alone in their enthusiasm about their own performance. They envision themselves in Runnymeade Meadow in 1215 presenting King John with the **Magna Carta** (with the role of King John assigned to their students.) Unfortunately, to their students, it is a long, drawn out gabfest.

Plan your presentation well. Keep your list of rules short. Add humor. Get to the point. State things clearly and simply. Add humor. Give a written bullet-point summary of the academic expectations. Add humor.

Post rules. Ask students to repeat back what they hear. Add humor. (As for all the procedural stuff, such as hall passes and sharpening pencils and taking care of the class pet garden gnome— you can spread those expectations out over the next few days.)

First Day
Teacher Perspective

By forging this great social contract, we are creating a bond that is the basis for all the great democracies.

Excuse me, Teach, but can I have a transfer?

Be ready to put the expectations to work that first day. Invariably some students will be inattentive or worse—disruptive. If this occurs, you have the perfect opportunity to DO what you said you would do and to review the expectation and consequences.

My First-Day Preparations

Before we leave the topic of how you make a good first impression, set the right tone, and effectively relay expectations at the beginning of the year, I'll share a discovery: A snappy visual presentation makes all this work so much better! So a few years ago, I began to use a PowerPoint presentation to engage my students in the information I wanted them to hear the first day. Here's how I prepare it and use it (you can skip over this if you'd rather talk or already have made your feature-length Day One film or just don't want to read any more about me):

1. First, I make my list of rules or expectations for behavior and relationships between the human beings in the classroom. (This is pretty easy. Most of us can think of plenty of offenses

that annoy us!) I pare those down to a reasonable number (three to five) and create a document. I check to be sure the rules are stated in positive terms and are behaviors students can actually do. I move on to consequences for inappropriate behavior. I write these down as well, ending up with a document of ONE page. I check to see that I have used bold, clear, concise language.

First Day
Student Perspective

Dude, summer is over! We just entered the gates of hell.

Article 10, section 15 of the class rules addresses cellphone usage on Mondays.

2. Next, I plan a sales pitch for my class. I want to make the class hard to resist. I draft a ONE-PAGE letter that tells students about the class. This includes paragraphs that tell something about me, describe content that will be studied, give a sneak preview of some typical learning activities, inspire the students to succeed, explain the grading-evaluation system, and summarize the class goals.

3. I polish the letter and the rules list and then direct my cursor to the PowerPoint icon. My goal is to present this information in a way that captures the students! I create a PowerPoint presentation for each of these purposes. One slide shows each part of the letter and each of the rules and consequences clearly. I try to add visual hooks, grabbing graphics, special effects, fun cartoons, Jim Sturtevant flair, and bizarre humor to the slides.

4. When slides are ready, I think about what I will say to add energy, humor, stories, and examples as I use the slides. This amounts to about a paragraph of "talk," with the exception of an occasional story. A dress rehearsal is a must! I'll practice in front of empty

You've Gotta Connect

desk, or perform in front of a mirror, or conscript some colleagues and offer a quid pro quo. Then I'm good to go.

5. I welcome students with my biggest smile. I embrace all the approaches and goals that I outlined earlier in the "Set the Tone" section of this chapter. With this thought foremost—"I will engage my students as I present this"—I project each slide and explain it thoroughly: the rules, consequences, introduction to me, introduction to the course, and introduction to our life together. I make eye contact with as many students as possible, relax, and share my enthusiasm for the great year ahead of us. My goal is to bring the information to life! I want students to relax and realize that this is going to be a safe environment. This is major groundwork for future relationships, and for a clear sense of what this class will be like. I take great pains to keep it from being long or boring. I don't want to put my students into a stupor. (Of course, I tell some stories—always the one coming up in this chapter about the fast-food adventure.)

A second great discovery was that I could use this same PowerPoint with parents! This has become the heart of my Parent Night presentations— and it works great. Parents tell me they feel they get a real picture of what will happen in my class for their child. And, this saves me tons of work! I've got that preparation all done! Even though I have sent the letter home to parents, they were happy to read another copy. (Not all those letters to the home actually got read! Fathers rarely read them.)

Follow **Get-Connected Action Steps 5.3 and 5.4** later in this chapter. These give guidelines and templates for creating your first-day presentations. Try **Get-Connected Action Steps 5.5 and 5.6** also. They suggest some activities that engage students in reflecting on, acting out, and explaining the expectations of the class. If you'd like more details on my own PowerPoint presentations, you can download samples from my website: www.jamesalansturtevant.com.

Survive Beyond Day One

Students need safety all year long. You can set the tone in the first few days and say all the right things to get off to a good start. It will mean nothing if you do not follow through on what you say.

I'll make this short. Many, many teachers have trouble with follow-through when it comes to all kinds of classroom expectations—behavioral and academic. Don't be one of them. Review and deepen understanding of the expectations throughout the first weeks of school. Hold to the procedures. Follow through without hesitation or loss of courage.

Go back and review the expectations you set for yourself. Do the Safety Check at least once a month. (See page 179). Engage students in conversation about these. Don't hesitate to ask students if they feel safe, if they understand the rules, or if they are experiencing the class as you described it on the first day.

Do a good job of teaching your students. Get kids involved in their own learning. Make sure lessons are dynamic, active, and relevant. Do a good job of supporting each kid and helping him or her feel like a real student. When a student gets a concept, increases a grade, masters a tough skill, or leaps over any academic hurdle, great strides in connection follow. In a school setting, nothing builds self-esteem, nothing builds trust from parents, nothing deepens relationships between teacher and student quite like academic success! This is a yearlong endeavor. Safety soars when students believe that you believe in them and know you are helping them to do well in school!

Listen to Students

The most disconnecting thing a teacher can do is to not be a professional.

You've Gotta Connect

Author's Reflection

My greatest epiphany about follow-through struck amidst French fries and spicy chicken. It was on a day when my wife and offspring were busy; thus I was on my own for dinner. School had been intense, so I headed to a local fast food joint right after school. It was early. I figured the place would be quiet. I spread out my food, pulled out a newspaper, and thought, "Ahhh, how nice!"

After a couple of bites and a few paragraphs, in walked the nightmare. Two preschool kids were screaming when they entered with their young mom. I had compassion for her. She seemed done-in! Now, I had been around other people's kids all day, and I wanted some peace; so I begged the forces of the universe, "Please don't let them sit by me!" Boom! We were the only customers in the entire restaurant, and they plopped down at the table next to me.

In about five seconds, chaos erupted. The little boy, covered with ketchup in record time, figured out how to squirt it at his little sister. The already-harried mom immediately became unhinged. She embarked on a litany of tactics. It started with yelling. This had no effect. Then came the threatening: "I'll take your milkshake away if you don't stop. I'll put you in the car if you don't stop." The kid ignored her.

Next, she started that infernal counting technique. You probably know this one. You've probably done it. The exasperated parent commands a child to stop; the kid continues; the parent starts counting "ONE, TWO, THREE..." You can see that the kid interprets this as, "You've got three seconds to continue doing this while you figure out what obnoxious thing to do next."

After about 20 idle threats, the mom lost it and smacked the kid on the rear, creating a big ugly scene.

Needless to say, my mellow meal was shot. Why would that poor kid take warning number 19 seriously? After you have been threatened so many times, you tune it out. Then all of a sudden—wham! I felt sorry for the kid and the mom. How is she going to influence him when he is 16? Wait! This kid will probably be in my class in 12 years! What will I do with him?

I left the place with indigestion and a new resolve to set clear expectations, outline clear consequences, and act. When inappropriate behavior pops up, I picture that fast-food scenario. It reminds me to point out the behavior, ask the student to stop, and if the behavior does not stop, ask "Are you refusing to comply with this request?" If the answer is silence or "yes"—the predescribed consequence goes into effect. No banter. No anger. Just follow-through. That is what is fair to the student.

Meet the Warm Demander

In the process of writing this book, I solicited some advice from an education professor at Otterbein University in nearby Westerville, Ohio. When I outlined my ideas, she responded, "It sounds as if you are describing a *warm demander.*"

As I was unfamiliar with the term, she suggested I google it. I did—finding thousands of links to *warm demander.* Judith Kleinfeld is credited with crafting the phrase in the mid-1970's when she was studying teachers in culturally diverse settings. As she identified teachers who succeeded in these situations, Kleinfeld used this phrase to describe what she believed to be their style of relating. **Warm demanders** are teachers who forge strong relationships with their students while simultaneously maintaining high standards.

Now, I'm not crazy about the word **demander**, although when paired with **warm,** it is intended to mean a nurturing, yet firm friend who holds you to standards. Still I wish the researcher had chosen something with a less aggressive and controlling feel. After all, it is the student who meets the expectations. The teacher is just the helper. So when I use the term, as Kleinfeld did, know that I am thinking of a *warm challenger* (or guide, booster, advocate, believer, or coach).

As I read about warm demanders, they popped into my mind left and right—teachers I know who just have that magic ability to forge strong bonds with students while holding them to high standards and pushing them to do (and be) their best. Of course, I know that this isn't magic. These teachers work at this! So I tracked some of them down and asked them to describe what it is they **DO**. For research on any topic, it's best to go to the primary sources. Unlike most original sources, these folks are very much alive and eager to share! Read about them, and be sure you complete **Get-Connected Action Step 5.7** to help with your own growth as a warm demander.

Start here

Nadine Adams has taught high school science for twenty-four years. She teaches Anatomy—a challenging subject that students must master if they plan on any type of career in the medical field.

> *During the first nine weeks, I learn about my students as they learn about me. It is a crucial time, as I am earning my students' respect and clarifying the behavioral and academic expectations I have of them. I also take the first step to stretch my boundaries while I sing to them or tell them a personal story in an effort to let them see me as a real person.*
>
> *Because I teach yearlong classes, I feel this makes me more effective as a warm demander. Early in the school year I am able to establish a positive relationship with my students, and I am able to build on this throughout the year. Just as biology content builds on itself and is interrelated, so the extent that I am able to*

"push" my students in learning also grows. I am able to more than gently push; I am able to warmly demand.

Laura Wood, now a middle school teacher, spent most of her 20-year teaching career instructing high school language arts. Her own childhood clued her in to the importance of relationships.

As a student I moved frequently—attending six school districts in four states during my K-12 career. I realized that while accents and ethnicities differed, the dynamics of schools were more similar than different. Feeling connected to my peers and teachers was vital to my emotional and academic survival. This is probably why I feel it is important to connect to my students.

I truly see myself as a coach-facilitator. I set up a disciplined, safe classroom atmosphere where students can take risks and are re-quired to reflect upon successes and challenges. I work for authen-ticity—as I know students have an innate appreciation of authentic-ity. (I remember as a student feeling annoyed when a teacher would praise something that I knew was undeserving of accolades.)

A respected colleague once advised me that my job was to "be seen, be known, and be gone." Giving students' ownership of their learning is vital. I feel most successful when students take over a discussion or are consulting with one another on writing revisions in organized, productive ways. I love it when they realize that I'm serious when I tell them to create a more challenging assignment to match my learning target. Too many educators underestimate what students can do. I want students to leave my classroom feeling that I did not waste a moment of their time.

You've Gotta Connect

Ted Van Tine has mastered a lot of roles in his long career: high school football coach, health and P.E. teacher, middle school science teacher, and athletic director. He started bonding with and inspiring kids in the fall of 1974—and is a master at bonding with reluctant students. He absolutely loves his job—and it shows.

Bo Schembechler, the legendary football coach at the University of Michigan, said it best, "Anyone can coach the willing!" I have always believed this applies to teaching as well. Anyone can TEACH the willing! The real skill is to motivate and teach those kids that aren't the best, brightest, or highly motivated. As a teacher, you have to be strong of character, high in motivation, have LOTS of energy, and most important—really like kids—ALL of them—especially the unwilling!

If connecting with kids is the real key to education (and I believe it is), then connecting with the "unwilling" is the real key in making a difference. It is not enough to "show them you care"—YOU HAVE TO REALLY CARE. (Kids are like sharks; they smell blood in the water and feed on the weak teachers. Kids also have an innate ability to sense a fake!) Call students by name, talk to them in the hall, sit with them at lunch and look for them to do things right! When they do something positive, recognize it!

Angie Stookesbury is a live wire—extroverted, a natural leader, and a highly visible member of her staff and community. In her 18 years as a high school English teacher, warm demander Angie *demands*, by example.

I genuinely love my job and my students. I want every one of my students to experience success.

Having a love for learning, I show my excitement every day in my classroom—even on days when I might not feel like it. If I'm not excited about what I'm teaching them, how can I expect my students to want to learn? I push my students to be the best they can be, and I continually push myself to become a better teacher each and every year. That's what we want our students to do, and they should expect nothing less from us. I hold myself to a high standard and my students know this. They see this in the classroom day in and day out.

Let's face it, we respond best to people who truly care about us and push us to become the best we can be. I overheard a group of students talking one day as I collected their essays. One student said, "I really didn't feel like writing this paper, but I didn't want to let Ms. Stooks down so I went ahead and wrote the thing." I can't tell you how happy that made me! I will definitely take a student who completes the work because I have built a relationship of mutual respect! My students know that I am prepared and ready to go every day. I expect nothing less from them. To be clear: It can't be all about the subject matter we teach. Students have to know that their teacher genuinely cares about them and their lives.

Georgia Craig has taught high school German for 21 years. Her students' AP Test scores are spectacular. She is a taskmaster, her curriculum is challenging, and she expects plenty of dedication and effort from students brave enough to take her course. But Georgia is all about connecting.

It is easy to get lost in content at the high school level. However, it is vital to remember that we teach students first and content second. Without connection and rapport with a teacher, students will only master so much academic material. It is my job to get to know my students—to identify their wants, needs, and abilities and to show them that I care by establishing high expectations not only for them but also for myself.

My classroom policies set the tone with my students with regards to forming high expectations. I begin my policies with a list of expectations for ME. It is important that students understand what they can expect from me or what the rules are for me to follow. Yes, I demand a lot from them too—it's a two-way street. I expect them to demand a lot from me.

I ask students to trust me to get them there. I tell them that learning German is a lot like running track. Sometimes I push them so hard that they are very uncomfortable and want to puke. But I will always be there to get them through their aches and pains and let them catch their breath so that they can keep going. I push students hard, but catch them before they fall. I show them how far they have come so that they can be proud of their accomplishments. After younger students see older students enter my classroom and speak German with ease and confidence, they want some of that.

Joe Cellar, six foot four inches tall and handsome, has presence. But he does not use his physical presence to intimidate. Instead he uses his warm personality and his outstanding sense of humor to put students at ease.

A 35-year coach once told me at his retirement: "It's not how much you know. It's how much you care." Any success I've had as an educator is attributed to this philosophy. It's all about letting the student know you're there to support them. How else does one motivate a 16- or 17-year old to learn microeconomics and macroeconomics? You make each day about them—not about you, not about the curriculum—it's about their needs. Yes, you lecture, but you connect the content to their lives. Yes, you ask them to graph, but you float around the room touching base with each student. Yes, you apply the learning, but you do it with an interactive game or assignment. In the process, you establish relationships—not "superficial small talk" relationships, but real "how's life?" relationships. You warm up to your students; they'll *warm up to you. Show an interest in them—and they **will** show an interest in what you're talking about.*

Skeptics will argue that you're being the student's friend rather than their instructor. How is showing an interest in your student's lives inappropriate for a student-teacher relationship? As long as your expectations and demands remain high, you're going to "kill it" in the classroom! I find students are actually more motivated to work for someone they can respect. That respect comes from the bond you've worked so hard to achieve.

In addition, I make sure my students see how hard I work. It's similar to being a boss in the working world: If your employees see you working your butt off, they're more likely to do the same for you. I teach AP Microeconomics and AP Macroeconomics. Exciting, right? (The enrollment rate has tripled in three years and AP exam scores remain above average.)

Elizabeth Curtis, eighth-grade Spanish teacher, would be the Judith Kleinfeld ideal: *an effective teacher in a culturally diverse setting.* Born in Nicaragua, Elizabeth finds that being a native speaker is a great benefit to teaching her predominantly Hispanic students (many of whom were not fluent in English). Working in a diverse urban setting, Elizabeth taught students who coped with poverty, crime, and low academic expectations.

I taught in an urban area in Miami, Florida, where most students had a low socio-economic status and came from foster homes. How in the world would I create an engaging classroom with this type of student population? Most of the self-help books for teachers were basically useless to me. Here are some things I had to learn on my own:

The first step to having a successful and engaging classroom in an urban school is CARING! Show students that you care and that you value their ideas, opinions, and them as a person. Most of these kids do not have a role model at home—or someone who cares enough about them to show that what they do and who they are matters. This is where their anger begins, and it extends to the classroom. Learn about your students. Empathize with their struggles. Only then you will gain their trust and respect.

A second critical step is positive reinforcement! To keep them from quitting, give encouragement and constant, constant, CONSTANT positive reinforcement! Many of these kids experience the opposite in their lives outside school—discouraging or berating comments. Many of their parents have little or no involvement in their academics.

*The third step is high expectations. Caring does not mean low expectations or lack of disipline. In my classroom, the **first** thing I do in the beginning of the year is to give clear expectations and hold to them consistently. They know that I care and that they can trust me. However, they also understand that what I say is what I mean. They know that I hold them to a high standard because I DO believe in them. And students clearly understand that if they do not deliver, consequences **will** follow. This breeds an unspoken mutual respect between teacher and students and it works. Students also appreciate and are more productive when the teacher is consistent with his or her expectations and holds them to higher standards.*

Jeanne Collett is not flamboyant, nor is she an extrovert. Warm demanders do not fit any certain mold. They are as diverse as the rest of humanity. Calm, pleasant, friendly, and patient—this 30-year old high school Chemistry teacher is unflappable. She has a real knack for reaching reluctant students and giving them confidence to make it through a subject that leaves many dazed and confused.

My demanding comes from my students knowing up front that I have content to teach them and that I have high expectations for their learning the material every day. They know I do not tolerate things like sleeping in class, using their phones, using their iPods while I am talking, doing other work during science class time, or choosing *to do nothing. These things are just unacceptable and they know this from the start of the year. This is the easy part of the **warm demander**.*

*The challenging part is the **warm**—and students will find learning hard without the teacher being warm. For me, being warm is how I connect with my students and how they connect with me. It is based on honesty, respect, and patience. I am open with my students about what I know, what I don't know, and who I really am. I don't make things up to pretend I know more than I do, and I don't alter my personality to become a different person in the classroom. I respect my students enough to listen to what they have to say about anything without judgment. I welcome their comments, suggestions, and stories. In return they respect me enough to listen to what I have to say and follow my classroom policies.*

*Patience is my most valued asset in teaching. I am a calm and collected individual. I know not every student is going to understand something the first time I present it. I might have to teach it ten different ways before some students understand. I am okay with that. Most importantly, I have the patience to wait for even the most difficult or stubborn students to come around. I will not give up on them. By the end of a school year these students are usually the students with which I have the deepest connections. Without the **warm**, students tend to go through the motions of the demands without really learning. I believe the **warm** is the most important key to a successful educator.*

It's time to practice. These action steps will raise the level of safety in your classroom, help you have a stellar first day of school, and move you along that path to becoming a great and warm demander (AKA coach, supporter, etc.). Then, don't neglect to finish the chapter by summarizing what you learned in the chapter. See the **Learning Targets Checklist** on the final page of Chapter 5.

Get-Connected! Action Steps

Action Step 5.1   Safety Inspection

Before the year or semester begins, it's a good idea to do a classroom safety check. Assume that the fire extinguishers have been replaced and the earthquake drill procedures are in place. Check YOUR plans, commitments, and preparation for assuring emotional, physical, and academic safety for your students.

1. What signs tell students that your classroom will be a safe place? Think about what you tell them the first day or week, who they perceive you to be, what they hear about treatment of each other in your classroom, and how you will help them succeed as students.

2. Using the **Safety Check** form on page 179, write your list of ways you want students to feel safe. You might write something like *safety from put-downs, freedom to learn at her or his own speed and level,* or *assurance that teacher will be his or her advocate.*

3. In the second column, write at least one action you commit to do to assure students of the safety you listed to the left.

4. Use the last column as a place to check or date when you feel you have a plan for addressing this safety need and have begun to implement it.

5. Come back to this list after a few weeks. Reflect on your safety record. Share it with students. Ask them to reflect back on it and tell how they think you are doing with this list. Ask colleagues for more suggestions for the "how to show it" column. Add more safety items to the list as you find more safety needs in your classroom.

Action Step 5.2 Listen In on First Impressions

As you begin to plan for your next school year or semester, think about these questions: What impressions do students have by the end of their first day or first week in your classroom? What impressions would you like them to have?

1. Make a copy of the **First Impressions Interview** form on page 180. Rewind your brain to last year. Pretend that you have just wrapped up your first day of class or classes. Assume that a student is asking her friend about your class. Complete this short interview, pretending to be a student who has just attended the first day in your class. Answer as a typical kid would answer.

2. If you are a student teacher and don't yet have teaching experience, think about a class you attended in the past, and complete the activity from memory. If you are working on the action steps with others, this is an awesome opportunity to pair up for some role-playing. Create a dialogue between the two imaginary students. Then, switch roles.

3. These are the kinds of basic questions students ask when interrogating a peer about a class and a teacher. Did you leave any questions unanswered? If you like what you wrote, great! This chapter will help you fine-tune the way you start off the school year. But if you are unhappy with your responses, or lack thereof, the action steps in this chapter can inspire your good preparations.

4. For any reply that is not satisfactory, restate it as you would like the student to answer. Envision this kid as very enthusiastic and eager to share excitement about your class. This is the way future students leaving your class the first day will respond!

Action Step 5.3 You'll Love This Class!

Design a sales pitch that will make students glad they landed in your class! Write a letter and send it home with students. But make sure students know what's in the letter! In this action step, you'll plan your sales pitch and get ready to share it with students and parents.

1. To "sell" yourself and your class, think about the inviting characteristics of both. Think about who you are and why you teach, what the class will offer students, what content students will learn and what kinds of activities will be used in their learning, how students will be evaluated, and what the great outcomes will be.

2. Use the **The Sales Pitch** form on page 181. Write thoughts and ideas for each of these areas. The first section is a place for you to write a great advertising headline or title, along with a short "hook" statement that will cause them to sit up and anticipate with eagerness what you'll say next. The last section is a place to jot some phrases or ideas about how you will wrap up your sales pitch with a bang!

3. Use the ideas from this form to write a letter to students. Write one paragraph for each of the seven topics. In the "Sell the Class" paragraph, give a hearty introduction to the kinds of strategies and activities students will enjoy as they learn. At the end of the letter, ask students and parents to sign at the bottom to show that they read this.

4. Use your letter as the basis for a PowerPoint or other visual presentation. Think about how you will present the information about your class to your students. They'll read the letter AFTER you have presented this to them in the first day or two of class.

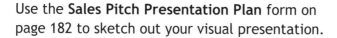

Use the **Sales Pitch Presentation Plan** form on page 182 to sketch out your visual presentation.

5. Present this to the students. The words on the PowerPoint slides, of course, will be just part of the presentation. Add cartoons. Involve your audience. Use humor. Start discussions. Finally, give students a copy of the letter. Review it with them. Ask them to sign that they read and understand it.

6. Send the letter home to parents via mail or email.

7. Use the PowerPoint presentation at your Parents' Night or Open House to review what your class will be like. Present it with the same flair and humor as you did with your students!

Action Step 5.4 What Can We Expect?

Think through all behaviors and attitudes expected in your classroom. Think about what students can expect from you. Think about what you expect of them in relationship to each other, to their schoolwork, and to you.

1. Use the **We Can Expect . . .** form on page 183 as you plan your school year and your first few days of school.

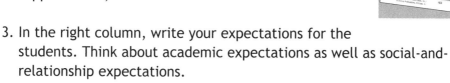

2. In the left column, write the commitments that you will make to your class. Identify what they can expect from you in the way you relate to them, support them, and teach them.

3. In the right column, write your expectations for the students. Think about academic expectations as well as social-and-relationship expectations.

4. At the bottom, jot down the consequences students can expect to accompany their honoring or dishonoring of expectations. Think about positive as well as negative consequences.

5. Plan to present this information to students in the most dynamic fashion possible. Use the ideas from the above activity to plan a presentation about expectations. How will you communicate these expectations to students? Prepare a visual presentation to help with that communication. Use the **Expectations: The Presentation Plan** form on page 184 to plan slides for a visual presentation. The words on the PowerPoint slides, of course, will be just part of the presentation. Add cartoons. Involve your audience. Use humor. Start discussions.

6. Use the PowerPoint presentation at your Parents' Night or Open House to review what your class will be like. Present it with the same flair and humor as you did with your students!

Action Step 5.5 What Did You Hear?

The first day of school can be a long haul for many kids. Often there is a lot of sitting and listening to rules and procedures. As you introduce them to both you and the class, get students up and moving. Try some of these activities to learn what the students actually absorbed from your efforts to let them know about class content, goals, and expectations. (Do some on other days in the first week or two to review and solidify procedures and expectations.)

1. Have groups create skits demonstrating unacceptable behavior and alternatives.

2. Let students do improvs (improvised comedy routines) to demonstrate expectations for social or academic behavior.

3. Conduct a mock press conference where a few students explain the content they will learn in this class.

4. Divide the class into small groups. Give each group a topic from a unit you've told them will be studied. Set a stopwatch or timer for five minutes. The group should record everything they already know about that subject.

5. Ask students to stand up with a pencil and notepad. Give them a limited time period, such as eight minutes. They must rotate around the room and hold a brief interview with five other students. The goal is to ask a question that will elicit ONE thing he or she did not know about that person. They record the student's name and the information. To avoid the problem where all the same kids get interviewed, make a rule that no person's name can show up more than four times on lists.

Action Step 5.6 How Do You Stack Up?

Revisit Action Step 3.2. By the time you completed that step, you have painted a portrait of the way you wanted students to view you and your class.

1. Review those ideas. How close are they to what actually happened at the beginning of the year or semester, and to what is happening now?

2. For an even better view of how you stack up, actually give the interview form to real students from your class(es). Use the **First Impressions Interview** form on page 180. Get an honest look at

how students experience you and the class in those early days. Now, how does this stack up to your goals?

Action Step 5.7 Grow as a Warm Demander

You've read the words of eight of my favorite warm demanders. (See pages 163-171.) You've been challenged to identify some warm demanders that you know. There is a lot to be learned from teachers who do this intentionally (and well). In fact, this is the very best place to learn a powerful skill.

1. Identify some warm demanders that you know personally. Contact at least one of them. Give the definition of a warm demander (see below and explain that you believe he or she is one.
   - *Warm demanders are educators who forge strong relationships with their students while simultaneously maintaining high standards.*

2. Make a copy of the **Growing as a Warm Demander** form on page 185. Ask your interviewee to respond to the prompt questions in part A. Take notes to identify key ideas or actions that you heard in the answer.

3. Re-read the personal comments from the eight teachers on pages 163 to 171.

4. Reflect on the advice from your interview and the teachers who spoke in this chapter. Complete B on the form.

5. Complete Part C on the form by setting some goals for yourself.

SAFETY CHECK

Students Will Feel Safe	How I'll Let Them Know	✓

179

You've Gotta Connect

FIRST IMPRESSIONS INTERVIEW

Questions

1. Hey, you just left _____'s class. What did you think?

2. What's (he) (she) like?

3. What are you going to learn in this class?

4. Is this class going to be hard?

5. What are the expectations for students in the class?

6. What can you expect from (him) (her) as a teacher?

Answers

1: My first impression is:

_____
_____
_____

2: Well, _____ is definitely

_____
_____
_____

3: _____ told us

_____
_____
_____

4: _____ told us

_____
_____
_____

5: We're expected to

_____
_____
_____

6: _____ said we could expect

_____
_____
_____

180

THE SALES PITCH

A Great, Grabbing Title: _____

The Hook: _____

Feature the Teacher: _____

What You'll Learn: _____

Sell the Class: _____

The Work Load and Grades: _____

The Rewards: _____

The Wrap-Up: _____

You've Gotta Connect

SALES PITCH PRESENTATION PLAN

Sketch out the plan for each slide in your presentation.

TITLE: _____

THE HOOK:

FEATURE THE TEACHER:

WHAT YOU'LL LEARN:

WHAT YOU'LL DO:

GRADING:

GOALS:

WRAP-UP:

WE CAN EXPECT...

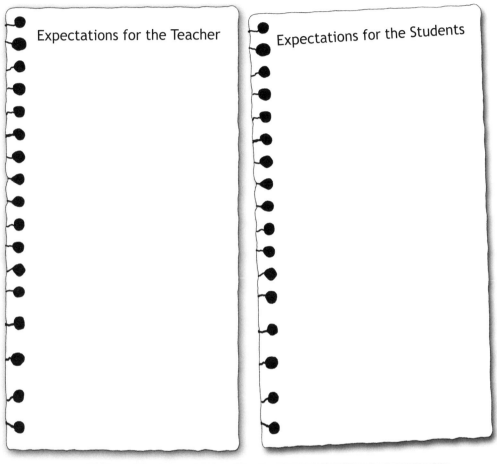

Expectations for the Teacher

Expectations for the Students

Consequences

You've Gotta Connect

EXPECTATIONS: THE PRESENTATION

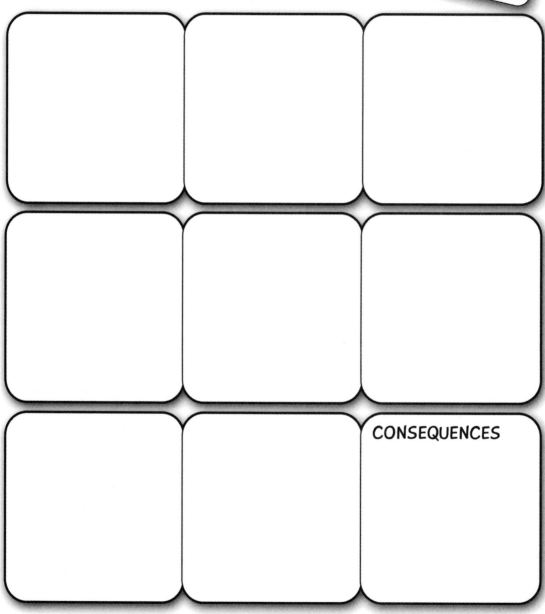

Sketch out the plan for each slide in your presentation.

CONSEQUENCES

GROWING AS A WARM DEMANDER

A. The Interview

Ask this question of at least one warm demander:
How do you forge strong relationships while simultaneously
maintaining high standards? What is your secret?

B. What do warm demanders DO?

From your interview and the real-life examples in this chapter, identify
at least eight specific actions taken by warm demanders:

C. What can you DO?

Circle four of the ideas from B that you can practice or improve.
Then answer these questions:

When will you begin these actions?

How will you evaluate your efforts?

When will you evaluate your efforts?

You've Gotta Connect

Learning Targets Checklist

To summarize what you have learned in this chapter,
check ✓ if you . . .

_____ have a plan to help your students feel physically and
emotionally safe in your classroom.

_____ are able to name at least ten actions you do throughout
the year to assure students they can be free from threat
as they learn in your classroom.

_____ have received student feedback about what it is like to
be in your class, including whether they feel safe.

_____ can show that you have communicated behavioral and
academic expectations and consequences clearly to
students.

_____ have made plans to be stellar at following through on
pre-determined consequences.

_____ can explain several ways that you assist and support
students in keeping or reaching academic and behavioral
expectations.

_____ have identified and worked on steps to grow as a warm
demander.

_____ can verify that you have completed most of the Get-
Connected Action Steps in this chapter.

Chapter 6

Enjoyment

If You're Not Smiling, You're Not Connecting

Each September, students in my Ancient History class squirm with angst when I tell them they'll be performing Greek dramas. The squirm turns to all-out anxiety when they learn that the dramas will be videotaped and shown to other classes.

I describe the format of the performance for the students. In the Greek dramas, some actors perform the role of the chorus, or narrators. My conscripted Greek chorus members get nervous at the prospect of chanting their lines. But usually, a few hams emerge who have no qualms about jumping into the chorus roles.

Students are assigned to groups. Groups organize themselves and then anxiously wait while I circulate around the room, assigning the dramas randomly. By this time I have explained that, though some Greek dramas are comedies (e.g., *Trojan Women*), most are tragedies (e.g., *Oedipus Rex*).

However, I know what's going to happen before we even begin rehearsals: Regardless of which scripts the groups receive, all their performances will turn into comedies. As a matter of fact, the students will put as much effort into making the plays funny as they will into fulfilling the assignment. I can also rely on ample doses of violence as their primary vehicle for the humor. Violence is easy to incorporate in Greek dramas.

The Greek drama has become a favorite tradition in my classes. I know that every year on show day students will pile into class bursting with youthful exuberance. They will be in costume, full of nervous energy. Many of the dramas will be hilarious. The funny presentations will have the biggest impact, and the actors will thoroughly enjoy themselves. The value goes far beyond the fun, creativity, and acting experience; the history, the content, and the morals of the stories will be etched in everyone's memory for decades. I'll get a warm feeling when I look around the room. I'll see the kids smiling, engaged, connecting, and **learning**. This is why I became a teacher!

Anyone who's been in a classroom for long knows the magic of humor in that setting. Kids gravitate toward it. When I ask students how teachers show acceptance of students or what teachers can do to connect to kids, the most frequent answers have something to do with humor. These are typical answers:

- I feel accepted by a teacher who makes kids laugh.

- A teacher who laughs and makes jokes is a good connector.

- The best way for a teacher to connect is to laugh at students' jokes.

- I feel connected to a teacher who laughs with ALL the students.

- When a teacher uses the students' jokes, he portrays students' ideas as relevant.

- My connection to one teacher grew when she comically defended me for something awkward I did.

- A teacher who relaxes and enjoys the students increases connection.

The Pitch

You connect with students when you use and allow humor. You connect with students by being human. You connect with students by enjoying them and helping them enjoy learning and living in your classroom. You spend a significant part of your life at school, with your students. So why not make this as enjoyable an experience as possible? Let's create a life where the working portion of our lives is a blast!

Students are drawn to happy teachers. Think back to your own school experiences. Certain teachers loved their work, and you reveled in the upbeat atmosphere in their classes. I can bet that two things were present in those classrooms: humor and a teacher who seemed human. When you welcome humor into your classroom, you'll watch connections deepen. When you enjoy your students and show them that you are human, you'll be delighted at the growth in the kinds of relationships that help kids succeed.

I'm a funny guy, but I don't think every teacher must be a standup comedian. Every teacher should, however, try to create a culture where students are relaxed and happy. Most things work better in such an environment. There is greater camaraderie. Kids feel safer. There are fewer behavior problems. More kids get more accomplished. So does the teacher.

This chapter will help you master the fine art of bringing humor and humanity to your classroom—in positive and appropriate ways. You'll find ways to add humor to your own presentations and dialogue. You'll learn about the benefit of sharing some personal stories with students. Most classes include some witty students. (Some of them are witty to the point of distraction or trouble.) You'll get some ideas for building relationships to those class clowns too. I agree that education is serious business, and teachers deserve to be viewed with respect. This chapter is not about destroying your image; it's about using humor constructively. There is no attempt to turn you into a court jester. Instead, the goal is to create an enjoyable setting where you and your students connect.

For this chapter on a classroom climate of **enjoyment**, your learning targets are:

Learning Targets

1. Add humor to your lessons, assessments, routines, and conversations.

2. Make progress with telling jokes and sharing personal stories.

3. Use fun signature phrases to add humor to classroom life.

4. Distinguish between appropriate and inappropriate classroom use of humor.

5. Learn some ways to embrace and manage those class clowns.

6. Increase your own enjoyment of your students and life in your classroom.

Find 1,000 Ways to Laugh

Yes, there are at least 1,000 ways and reasons to laugh in your classroom. Dozens of opportunities abound each day. Even more important, there are many reasons why teachers and students should laugh together. Any experienced teacher who allows laughter regularly in the classroom could make a list of reasons. If you need research to be convinced about the "why," read some of the resources included on page 276.

Humor in the classroom

- helps teachers get and maintain students' attention

- engages students in classroom life

- inspires students to pay attention to lessons

- eases awkward social contacts

- defuses potentially explosive situations

- ignites motivation

- nurtures creativity

- fights apathy

- wakes kids up

- can change the subject

- can rescue a dull moment

- shows that teachers are human

- distracts from hostilities, disappointments, and problems

- breaks down barriers

- relieves stress

- eases drama or trauma

- helps the brain learn and retain ideas

- helps to reduce discipline problems

Ask Yourself:

Do I have a good laugh with students in every class every day?

Many students actually want to go to a class where there is laughter. If you need any more research to be convinced that humor belongs in every classroom, just do a survey and tally up the results. Ask this question of your students and your own children: "Which teacher would you prefer to have—one that tells jokes, welcomes humor, and shares some wacky personal stories or one who wants a perpetually calm, serious classroom and does not let students know anything about his or her personal life?"

So here are a few of the ways you can add humor to your classroom:

1. Post quips, jokes, puns, funny sayings, cartoons, or comic strips around the room, on the class website, in the class newsletter, or on the door.

2. Add puns, riddles, or cartoons to study guides, practice sheets, and things you project.

3. Write funny, clever examples on quizzes and tests.

4. Share funny news stories, articles, or headlines to start class.

5. Tell brief, humorous (though perhaps mundane) stories about your life experiences.

6. Regularly include these in your lessons or presentations: puns, amusing or surprising stories, fun mnemonic techniques, tongue twisters, jokes, idioms, and cartoons.

7. Add appealing or amusing visuals to your classroom. Use clever posters or outlandish decoratives.

8. Welcome student jokes (appropriate ones, of course) and other forms of humor.

9. Encourage students to share fun stuff they hear, see, or read. Work as a group to make up riddles, puns, oxymorons, jokes, tongue twisters, poems, raps, or silly songs that explain or review a concept that students are learning.

10. Don't take yourself too seriously. Laugh at yourself. Laugh at your idiosyncrasies and mistakes.

11. Be spontaneous with humor. As long as it is appropriate and non-disruptive to the learning, you can't go wrong to inject humor. (Don't expect kids to laugh at everything you think is funny, though.)

12. Don't let a day go by without a hearty laugh with your students—in every class.

As you use and encourage appropriate humor, take opportunities to discuss the topic with students. They'll see you as a model. But in addition, talk straight about what's appropriate and what's not, about what's disruptive and what works along with a program where learning is taken seriously.

Tell Jokes

I'll begin by telling a joke that I repeat every year in my Economics class. We study a unit on money—the creation of money, the nature of money, the history of money, and the role of money. It's an abstract unit, and I like to lighten the atmosphere with this lame joke about counterfeiters. Here is the *Reader's Digest* version (figure of speech only—not actually **from** the *Reader's Digest*):

> *This not-so-intelligent guy decides to become a counterfeiter. He makes a number of $15 bills. His friends warn him that he will never get away with trying to pass a $15 bill. Undeterred, he decides to go a convenience store where he knows the clerk and believes she is none too swift. He buys a candy bar. He is thrilled when the clerk accepts his fake money and gives him change! He's rather self-satisfied when he reports his success to his friends. He is so proud that he even shows off the change he got—which consists of a 30-cent piece, two $3 bills, and a $6 bill!*

It's a cheesy joke, but when I first heard it years ago, I immediately recognized its huge potential for my class. I used the joke recently (much longer version), and it took 12 minutes to tell! Say what?

Here's how I told it: I began with some background about a couple of buddies working on an assembly line who were worried about downsizing. (At this point, my students have no idea that this is a joke because we discuss such issues every day.) So, one decides he is going to start **making money**. I go on a bit with the semantic confusion associated with the phrase "making money." Students are beginning to question the veracity of the story, but I push on. I do a dramatic presentation where one friend visits the counterfeiter to see what he has been up to. A mini punch line comes when the counterfeiter hands the fake bill to the friend. I produce what looks like a bill of some sort. I examine the paper closely then look at the

Ask Yourself:

Have I seen a joke ease a tense situation?

You've Gotta Connect

students in a confused fashion. I do this a number of times. I then announce that it is a $15 bill with myself (impersonating a president) pictured on it. I show the bill around the room.

The class responds pretty well to this and thinks that I have delivered the punch line. I can even sense some relief, but we are not yet to the halfway point!

I go into a lot of dramatics about the dynamics between the counterfeiter and the friend. The counterfeiter refuses to go back to his existence of hourly work on the assembly line. This all leads up to the actual joke. I act out, with nervous tension, walking into the convenience store and purchasing the candy bar with fake money. Finally, I hit them with the climax when phony bills and coins are produced from my pocket.

It is quite a performance that leaves my audience a bit shocked and fatigued. There is generally some nervous laughter. My students snicker about the whole scenario for the rest of class period.

The joke has become legendary at our school. Many students who sat with their mouths open during the performance, ask for an encore. Former students ask me for a replay 10 years after they graduate. Younger students beg me to tell it to their class. I honor none of these requests.

Many times I have been asked, "Isn't telling a 12-minute joke a waste of class time?"

My answer is an emphatic "NO!"

Many students try to recreate the joke at home and report blank stares on their victim's faces. They always come back and tell me about their experiences. I let them know that the joke is even more fun to tell than it is to hear. That 12 minutes is not wasted. It creates a common memory every one of us in the room can share. No kid has come to me and told me the joke was awful and I should never do it again, and I have been telling the joke for 15 years. Over a thousand kids have been subjected to it.

I'm not recommending that you spend 12 minutes every day on a joke. Do this once in a while. If you want to tell more jokes, there are plenty of short tales, riddles, puns, one-liners, or two-liners that you can tell. Here are three of my students' favorites. The first two are homemade jokes. The third is borrowed and well known. All three have some remote connection to my subject area, social studies. All three follow in the "lame joke" tradition that kids love.

Q: *What do you call an illegal alien in Sweden?*
A: *An artificial Swedener*

Q: *Why are people in Taiwan stressed out?*
A: *Because they have Taipei personalities*

Q: *Did you hear that the world's best farmer is from Ohio? (my state)*
A. *Yes, I heard he's outstanding in his field.*
   (Often my most intelligent students don't get this one for a while. They read too much into it. "Oh—what's his specialty?")

Of course the point of all this is to encourage you to tell jokes. Even if you're not a seasoned joke-teller, give it a try. See **Get-Connected Action Step 6.1** later in this chapter for some help preparing to tell a joke.

Capitalize on Fun Phrases

In high school I had a science teacher who was a decent instructor, but was not the most animated person. I forgave him because I thought he had a topic to teach that was less than thrilling. I went to class and did my "student thing" every day with little excitement or anticipation. (I find that most students go to a majority of their classes in a similar mindset.)

To my surprise, something interesting happened in that class as the semester progressed. My friends and I noticed that the teacher would bust out some peculiar lines on an increasingly regular basis. Chief among them was the innocent statement, "Let's go back to the map!" This rather dull phrase was delivered with such gusto that it caught us completely off guard—every time. He didn't just state it. It came out in the form of a dramatic song. His voice emphasized "LET'S," and then he trailed off and said the word "map" with a normal tone. It was more like:

"LET'S.............go back to the map!" He put this forth with emphasis and flair. It almost took as long to say the word "LET'S" as the other five words in the sentence. It was a fantastic attention grabber.

My friends and I got to the point where we would smile and snicker every time he said it. We would also ask questions to elicit the response. Did he catch on to our little game? Probably. He seemed to enjoy it as much as we as we did; this actually got him smiling. These episodes made the class more enjoyable. Reflecting back, I realize the guy was a good teacher. I **connected** with him more than I had known then—all because of that stupid little phrase.

Do I have signature phrases? Oh yes, and in my classes "LET'S........ go back to the map!" is bellowed on a daily basis. I am a social studies teacher and thus keenly aware of the past. I love to reminisce in order to make connections with the present. Often these stories are personal in nature. When I introduce one of those memories, I do it with one of my most popular phrases. I always lead with the season and the year: "It was the **FALL** of 1976!" I bust out the "**FALL**" in a loud dramatic voice. My students look at me and think, "Okay, what happened in the fall of 1976?" (Think of the late great Paul Harvey with his signature "and now............the **REST** of the story!" Think of Paul if, that is, you are old enough to have a clue who Paul Harvey was.)

Listen to Students

There's nothing like accepting someone who acts as though he really wants to teach you.

Here are a few more examples:

- I always refer to my wife as the "The Lovely Mrs. Sturtevant."

- When it is time to shift gears, I almost always say, "At this point in the space-time continuum."

- When a student correctly answers a difficult question, I point to the youngster and warble, "All over it like a cheap suit!"

- When I introduce a controversial topic, I sit back in my chair and proclaim "Buckle Up!" At the same time, I reach over my left shoulder and pretend to grab, then secure, a seatbelt. It is a great attention-grabber.

- To start ancient history class I rarely say, "Pull up a chair." Instead I say, "Pull up a CHARIOT!"

These phrases draw the listener in. In many ways they are irresistible. Last year, one of my students made a *Sturtevant Time Line* based on my "season/year" introductory phrase. Over the course of the semester, he made marks along a line that began in 1961, the year I was born, and ended in the fall of 2012. It was remarkably accurate. He made copies and gave it to the rest of class. I was flattered, and the other students thought highly of him for doing it. He and I developed a strong bond that continues because of a ridiculous little dramatic intro to my personal stories.

Signature verbalizations are not always sentences or phrases. Sometimes there is just a word that you use again and again. I try to choose a new one every semester. My current word is *copious*. I use *copious* throughout the day. I never define my signature words. I leave it up to the students to look them up. All they have to do is listen to the context and they generally figure it out. When I see kids in the hall or outside of school, I am amazed by how many will shout out the word *copious* in some bizarre context.

Before you can capitalize on your speech patterns or use them with style, you must become aware of them. **Get-Connected Action Step 6.4** later in this chapter guides you to identify these verbal habits and use them well.

This step will also challenge you to drop or adapt habits that are not having positive effects. (For instance, I've become aware that I overuse the word *NOW*. I use it for punctuation. I finish one set of instructions and then bust out the "NOW" to signify the next directive. I was unaware that I did this, but now am determined to rein in this annoying habit.)

Add Wisdom

I say "Yes! Yes! Yes!" to humor. Be aware, however, that there are some definite "No-No's" that must accompany your use of humor in the classroom. You've got to use wisdom along with the humor! The rule of thumb should be "appropriate"—but I'll elaborate even further, just in case you may not think of the following cautions as part of your judgments about "appropriate." Here are six "No-Nos" for teachers:

1. Never use sarcasm (not even with high school kids). Sarcasm, by its very nature, is hurtful. Merriam Webster defines this as *"a sharp and often satirical or ironic utterance designed to cut or give pain."* If you look up definitions in a dozen dictionaries, you will find descriptors and synonyms such as *harsh, mocking, contemptuous, ridicule, scorn, insult, caustic, wounding, derision, bitter, taunt, sneering*. However it's defined, sarcasm has no place in the classroom.

How often do I use sarcasm with my students?

I'll go on a bit more about sarcasm here, because it is such a widespread tactic used by teachers. It is so easy to resort to sarcasm in the face of frustration. For many teachers, it is a staple of their repertoire. Here is a typical scenario:

Teacher: *"Hey Johnny. Do you have your assignment?"*
Johnny: *"No! I was too busy texting my girlfriend."*
Teacher: *"Wow! That is really going to prepare you to compete in the global economy."*

Everyone laughs at Johnny and his attitude. Johnny even laughs. But even though Johnny enjoys his rebellious reputation, he knows that the teacher just dissed him. He understands that this is now part of the relationship with the teacher, and he will return the favor. Worse, the teacher just reinforced a negative image of this student to the entire class. All the other students are now on notice that this teacher has no problem making them look bad in front of their peers. (Sadly, the teacher reinforced the insecurities buried beneath Johnny's arrogant exterior.) Is this the kind of atmosphere you want to create?

2. Resist the temptation to use sarcasm. Don't allow students to use it.

3. Allow no jokes about disabilities, weight, body type, gender, nationality, ethnicity, religion, sex, sexual orientation, suicide, or other death.

4. Don't permit students to laugh **at,** make fun of, or belittle anyone. (This includes people who are not present.)

5. Watch out for put-downs. These can be subtle. Make your class a "No Insult Zone."

6. Do not initiate, join in, approve, condone by ignoring, or laugh at any of the above.

7. Be alert! Pay attention to how kids respond to humor. Some kids are more sensitive than others. Even if you can argue that a use of humor is appropriate, it is not appropriate if it makes a student uncomfortable.

DO have discussions with students about humor. Nurture the understanding that humor is for fun, enjoyment, relaxation, and to make people feel good. Make it clear that you won't allow any humor that hurts or demeans an individual or group. See **Get-Connected Action Step 6.5** later in this chapter for an exercise on humor do's and don'ts.

Tell Personal Stories

My head hit the pillow a bit later than I'd planned on that Wednesday night. For me, Wednesday night is an important night for shut-eye. If I don't get a good night's sleep on Thursday night, I can suck it up and make it through Friday. But on Wednesday night, with two full days left in the week, I need that educational mojo.

By 2:14 on Thursday morning, I was deep in slumber dreaming about something delightful. My dreams were shattered by a frightening noise. After some temporary terror, I figured it out. There are tons of squirrels on my wooded property. They often run on the roof, but this time one had crawled into my attic and was doing little doughnuts at warp speed about 7 feet above my head. I am very fortunate to have an excellent spouse who is no shrinking violet. We decided to tackle the problem, which was going to take some effort.

Does this sound like a happy moment? It wasn't. But even at the time, I told Penny that we'd laugh about this in the future. Eureka! The future would be just hours away in my first period class, I realized! I grabbed our digital camera and became a photojournalist.

The first step in the process was to get my varmint trap out of the garage. Now I am a humane person (as I assured my students when I told the story); the trap is designed to capture the critter without hurting it. It was the dead of winter, so I knew the squirrel would be hungry. What squirrel can resist peanut butter? Not one that I know.

The next step was to set up the ladder. My house is a long ranch with the attic entrance on one side and the squirrel firmly ensconced at the other end above my bedroom. This was a huge problem, because my attic is nothing more than a crawl space. I had to act like a squirrel and climb from rafter to rafter. It was a great workout, but I am not in the Marine Corps and don't enjoy being roused and forced into combat.

Next, the brave explorer ascended to the attic. I was armed with the trap and a flashlight. I was a little concerned that the frightened creature might attack me. My adrenaline was pumping, and I was ready for war. But if the beast had struck, I probably would have lost my balance and fallen through the drywall ceiling of the main floor.

At last, the trap was laid in a bed of insulation. Not once did I hear, see, or smell the beast. But I can tell you that during the whole process, if anyone had snuck up behind and touched me or even said, "Boo!" I would have spontaneously combusted.

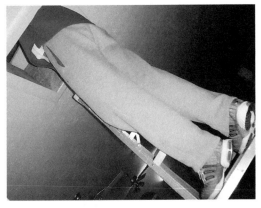

With a passionate voice and a bit of arm waving, I recreated the situation for my students the next morning. To augment the story, I projected the trusty images of the adventure on the classroom SmartBoard.

The following day my students demanded a "squirrel report." Some of my students were concerned about the squirrel. I felt the same. If a squirrel gets caught in one of those traps, you have to get it out quickly or it will freak out and hurt itself trying to escape. I believed I would hear the squirrel if it got stuck, but

You've Gotta Connect

I did not hear a sound for the rest of that night or the next. I climbed back up the next morning and found nothing.

Students wanted to hear the "squirrel report" every day until the crisis was resolved. See how they got drawn in to the story? For the rest of the week, students came to class with their own varmint reports. Some retold my story to rave reviews at their family dinner tables. I got no complaints from students about hearing the story. When I saw parents in town, a few stopped me and said how much they enjoyed their kid's rendition of the "squirrel report." Generally that was followed by some expression of gratitude that I seemed to connect with their child.

You're wondering about the squirrel, aren't you? I checked that trap morning and evening for a week. I never found the squirrel. Finally I took the trap out of the attic. The squirrel lives.

Try to tell some sort of a personal story about once a week. It doesn't have to be long. It does not have to be earth shattering. When you get a lot of feedback or stories of their own, you know you have struck gold!

You can re-tell anything (appropriate) that gives a glimpse into your life—what you do, what your interests are, what you do with your family—even what you eat. Weekends supply plenty of material. This past weekend my wife and I had a date. It was a Saturday night, and our children were with friends, so we actually got to go out by ourselves. We went to Costco, Home Depot, and Wal-Mart; then we had dinner at Chipotle. We capped it off with desert at Graters Ice Cream. Sound hot? My students didn't think so, but they laughed when I confessed to middle-aged squareness. I told them that I am their future. They responded with looks of horror.

Tell stories. Add pictures. Stories are connecting. See **Get-Connected Action Steps 6.2 and 6.3** later in this chapter for some help preparing to tell a story.

Author's Reflection

When I encourage my colleagues to share trivial aspects of their lives with their students, many are reluctant. They give such responses as:

"That would be embarrassing!"
"No one would be interested!"
"My students would think I'm an idiot!"

These sentiments are understandable. But as I ponder them, I realize that sharing trivial aspects of life is the status quo for young people. Most of them do this constantly through social networking. This is the way our students communicate! It's what they like. It's what they expect. Facebook and Twitter are all about sharing the ordinary happenings—as well as some pretty personal details. It seems that little is kept private.

On social networking sites, students inform their friends (and the entire world for that matter) about: their latest crushes or romances; what they watched on television; their favorite movies and music in the form of video clips. They post massive photo albums of themselves and endlessly report trivial details about their daily existence. There are thousands more users of online social networks who don't even post but are big-time lurkers (people who follow social networking discussions and messages but do not post themselves). Young people also share all kinds of mundane and personal information through texting and a variety of instant message opportunities. So I tell my colleagues, "Don't worry. Your students are totally down with receiving information of the kind you'd share in your stories."

Connect with Care

I was a big fan of the 1960's sci-fi series "Star Trek," primarily because I had a mad crush on Lt. Uhura (miniskirts and black boots as a functional military space uniform—really?), but also because I loved the stories. The main characters always made a big deal out of Starfleet's prime directive:

There can be no interference
with the internal development of alien civilizations.

When it comes to utilizing social media, educators need a prime directive:

Don't post anything you couldn't display
in class on your SmartBoard.

Unlike Kirk and Spock, who broke "Star Trek's" prime directive almost every episode and kept their jobs, you could lose yours if you do any of the following:

- become Facebook friends with your students

- follow any of your students on Twitter

- text or e-mail your students ANYTHING inappropriate

- post images of yourself consuming alcohol or drugs

- post images of yourself scantily clad or in any seductive poses or poses that someone—with a wild stretch of the imagination—could claim to be seductive

- in a fit of youthful indiscretion, display on a site any body parts that are generally covered

- take strident stands on controversial issues

- make politically incorrect references and jokes (particularly anything that includes Nazis)

Some teachers make the mistake of thinking that what they do on social media is their business. Alas! If you post it, you've made it the world's business. So, be smart. Ask yourself before you post, "Could I, would I, display this to my students in class?" If the answer is "no," BACK AWAY FROM THE SEND BUTTON! Follow the prime directive and keep your job.

This is not just about keeping your job. Nor is it just about cyberspace contacts. When I titled this section "Connect with Care," I meant, "Be careful about how you connect with students." There is always a fine line to walk for sharing information, thoughts, questions, experiences, stories, opinions, and gestures with your students. Technology just explodes the possibilities for crossing the line carelessly and inappropriately.

Teachers show disconnection when they are not passionate about their work.

Share your stories with students, but stay away from the most personal matters. There are many adult matters that are not the business of young people—especially if they are your students. Share the fun, silly, harmless, mundane stories that show you are human—and maybe a little bit nuts (in a good way)!

Embrace the Class Clown

Many teachers cringe when they hear "humor in the classroom" because it brings to mind the class clown—the scourge of serious learning. First of all, I want to note that not all class clowns are problematic. Some kids are just delightfully funny and have skills to use their humor without harm or disruption. However, there are class clowns that seem to be "the scourge" because teachers just do not know how to deal with them. In the past, many class clowns have faced frightening consequences. (Back in the day, they probably took the brunt of the corporal punishment meted out at the principal's office.) But regardless of the consequences, every school still had class clowns. It is not

You've Gotta Connect

acceptable to violate the Geneva Convention, so let's explore a better way to live with the class clown.

Teaching is a tough existence if you are at odds with your students. You can learn to welcome them, appreciate their humor, and keep them from disrupting or dismantling classroom plans or relationships. I'll share some tips that I have learned from working at this challenge.

But Mr. S., you said you loved my sense of humor.

The most effective way to **manage** class clowns is to connect with them (surprise, surprise—that "C" word again!). Education would be a dull enterprise without their humor. Embrace that they exist, and try to get them on your side. You will elevate and enjoy the use of humor significantly when you connect with and manage your pranksters.

So, how do you do it? As with other discipline challenges, you set expectations, anticipate problems, strive for consistency, follow through with consequences when needed, and constantly work at a relationship with the clown. The better you connect, the more of a joy and asset her or his humor will be to the class.

Distractions from class clowns generally fall into three categories:

The Class Clown **Big 3**

1. general disruptions

2. sarcasm

3. derisive statements directed at other students, or you

The first step is to identify and anticipate the behavior. Most of us handle issues better if we have time to think about proper responses. Sometimes you have to think on your feet, but even then, it's helpful to know what could be coming. Avoid pulling the disruptive students out in the hall for a private "Come to Jesus" or "I am going to set you straight" talk. Even more, avoid giving the talk in front of peers. Most pranksters have been through this drill many times. Usually those "talks," appeals, or threats have not worked. Any "getting into trouble" that is public just elevates their status as the premier class clown.

The second step will be to build rapport with the class clown and hold him or her to pre-arranged expectations in class, during instruction. Your role as teacher, your skill at connecting, and your homage to the class expectations will be enhanced—in front of all students.

For the third step, you will make contact with the class clown outside of class to work on a relationship of trust and care. This affirming follow-up communication deepens your connection.

Here are some scenarios to demonstrate constructive responses to troublesome class clown behaviors.

General Disruptions

Let's say you have a student who is a good kid, but she is ornery. The rest of the class gets a big kick out of her sense of humor. It is not her comments as much as her timing. She tends to blurt things out at inappropriate times. If it happened every once in a while, it would be no big deal, but that is not the case. It is frustrating and distracting. It is obvious that she is testing your boundaries.

Before class, you anticipate that your lesson may lead to some of her outbursts. You map out your strategy. Predictably, the next day in the midst of instruction, it happens: "Mr. _____, I read that pirates were constantly in search of booty!" This play on words is

You've Gotta Connect

funny and the class responds. You are biting your lip too. Sometimes your students say really funny things. Try not to laugh! If you do, it is like dumping gas on an open flame.

You seize this opportunity, and in a friendly tone you reply, "Marta, that is really witty! I love your sense of humor, but you are interrupting the class. Please don't do that. I will not interrupt you when you are making important points." You affirm her, but at the same time, you communicate your expectations. If she interrupts again (as the class clown usually will), assign the consequences that everyone knows are the rules of the class. Lay down the law in a cheerful, calm way. This method is very successful with most jokesters. Anticipate situations, create a plan, and keep your cool!

Now the work begins. Look for any opportunity to have a positive interaction with Marta. When she uses humor in positive ways, be very responsive. If it's not the time to reward her for appropriate use of humor, just laugh. Tell her, "You know, you really crack me up!" She will put it together.

Once you establish a solid relationship with pranksters, their sabotage efforts diminish. They stop looking at you like an adversary and feel free to express their humor in appropriate ways. When they start sharing jokes with you before and after class, you have met the goal—relationship forged!

Sarcasm

You have a student who is very sarcastic. Sarcasm is so often hurtful that it is best to keep it out of your classroom altogether. You can teach students to understand and enjoy political cartoons that employ sarcasm or help them identify it as a literary technique. Those are only kinds of situation where sarcasm should show up.

> ### *Listen to Students*
>
> *When teachers tell stories about doing crazy things, I feel like they would understand the stupid things I do.*

You are prepared when your sarcastic student springs into action, "Mrs. _____, you know the only reason that we have to study civil rights is to be politically correct!" You respond, "Jason, sarcasm is a very advanced form of humor. In ancient Greece, the term meant literally, *to tear the flesh*. So, we have to be careful how we use it. I thought your last comment was inappropriate because it creates a false impression of the importance of this lesson. I love much of your humor, but that statement was unfair."

Your response affirms Jason in a calm, friendly tone, but you leave no doubt who is in charge. If he persists, you do what you do when any student disregards a classroom rule—you apply consequences. If you are careful with your tone of voice, you can avoid sending a belittling message to Jason or putting him down in front of his peers.

Then, once again, you have more work. Make contact (soon) with Jason. Show him that you want a relationship with him, that you enjoy his wit and humor, and that you want to help him use it for appropriate fun in the classroom. The reprimands are likely to decrease.

Derision

Too often, class clowns couch putdowns in humor. Be on the lookout for this and be prepared to act. This is verbal bullying. A classmate answers a question, and BAM! the bully strikes with, "Mr. _____, the only reason that she knows the answer is because she is a nerd and has no life!"

You respond in a calm, cordial manner, "Niki, I have always been impressed with how observant you are. I am also taken by your sense of humor. You say some really funny things. The last comment, however, was abusive. It is the kind of comment that is not tolerated here." You will need to use some professional judgment, because some comments warrant a consequence while others just a warning. Often hecklers will make derisive comments about their friends and the target finds the comments hilarious. Many of us have experienced being the butt of such statements. However, don't allow derision, even if the target thinks it's no big deal.

Make a strong effort to bond with students who have this unwelcome talent of derision. If you can break Niki of this annoying habit, she will find less abusive outlets for their humor. And, more importantly, the targets of her humor can catch a break!

Finally, later in the period or the next day, find a time for a private conversation with Niki. Explain that her comments may have really hurt someone. Encourage her to connect with an experience where she was derided. Suggest that she think about apologizing to the target of her comment, but don't force it. Sometimes a kid will apologize, sometimes they won't. Plant the idea anyway.

Keep in mind: The rest of the class may really enjoy the class clown's antics, in limited doses of course. That's fine as long as the humor is not disruptive or hurtful. You can help the class clowns find healthy outlets for their humor. Follow **Get-Connected Action Steps 6.6 and 6.7** for practice responding to and managing class clowns.

Ask Yourself:

Would my students say that I enjoy them?

Now put what you've learned to work. Follow the action steps to practice adding humor to your classroom and building the relationships that can flourish when students see you as human. Then, don't neglect to finish the chapter by summarizing what you learned in the chapter. See the **Learning Targets Checklist** on the final page of Chapter 6.

Get-Connected! Action Steps

Action Step 6.1 Joke-Telling 101

It is time to tell a joke in class. This may be uncomfortable, but give it a try. Don't worry! It can be short.

1. Try to choose or create one joke that is tied, at least remotely, to your curriculum. You may be wondering where you can find a joke. That is the easy part. Search the Internet. Try searching "math jokes" or "history jokes." You won't be disappointed in the volume, but you will definitely have to do some sifting to get a joke that is appropriate. You can also search for riddles, puns, or tongue twisters. These make good jokes and are easy to find or make up. All you have to do is make a play on a word in your content area.

2. The students should not be aware initially that you are telling a joke. Try to sneak into it as if it were just another part of the lesson. Then, be prepared for students not to laugh when you deliver the punch line. They may not get it. They may not find it funny. Don't worry about this in the least. Most kids will enjoy the joke even if they don't laugh, or even if they complain about it! Don't we work in a nurturing supportive profession? The key is, you told a joke.

3. If it feels comfortable, do it again sometime in the near future. Even if it was a bit uncomfortable, keep trying. Your students will love it.

4. After you've told the joke, reflect on the experience. Use the **Joke Reflection** form on page 218.

You've Gotta Connect

Action Step 6.2 Storytelling 101

You certainly have read enough of my stories in this book. If you are not already a teller of stories to your students, get ready to share a personal experience with your class. (If you're working through this book with colleagues, you can first try it out on them.)

1. Choose a funny incident, a frustrating predicament, an evolution of some sort, or something you witnessed. Tell the story from the standpoint of reflection—you looking back on what happened.

2. Explain what you learned from the whole scenario. From my "Squirrel Reports," my class can tell you I learned about my wife's impressive attitude and tenacity, as well as her good humor. (She is a warrior—one I'm glad to have in my foxhole!) Students also heard that I learned this lesson: You need to deal with annoying problems; procrastination is a bad idea.

3. Always allow time for your audience to talk about similar experiences.

4. After you've told your story, reflect on the experience. Use the **Story Reflection** form on page 219.

Action Step 6.3
Photo-Embellished Stories

Let's go further. It is time to take out your cell phone (or any other camera) and start snapping some pictures. There is no doubt: The images in the "Squirrel Report" made the story come to life.

You might be reluctant to take this step because you can't think of subject matter for pictures. Subject matter is not the problem; reluctance to share is usually the problem. Hey, if you are going to succeed in this business, or life for that matter, you have to develop some chutzpah!

Here is an easy one. Next time you go to a restaurant, take some pictures of your food. This past semester, my students loved our student teacher. At the end of his tenure, my wife and I took him out to dinner along with his significant other. We went to a popular steakhouse known for its delicious rolls. I often eat so many rolls that I barely consume the main course. You can bet that there were photos of the rolls, along with a roll-consumption inventory report. There were also pictures of my student teacher and his friend. The photo-embellished story was a big hit.

1. Start clicking pictures. If you take photos that you don't use, just delete them. It is not a big deal. It could be one shot or a series of images. You could take a before and after picture. How about the next time you get a haircut?

2. Use the experience and the pictures together to tell your story. Find a way to project the images or other way to share them with the entire class.

3. After you've told your story, you can use the same process to reflect on your story as you used in Action Step 6.2. Use the **Story Reflection** form on page 219. This time, evaluate your use of photos as a part of question #5.

Action Step 6.4 Signature Phrase Cache

Take a personal inventory of the words and phrases you use repeatedly. The purpose will be to find words or phrases that have a positive impact and weed out or alter those that are unhelpful, negative, or just plain annoying. I'll wager that you'll find this to be quite an enlightening experience.

1. Many people are unaware of their verbal patterns, so ask some students you trust to tell you about any words, phrases, or sentences you use habitually. Ask more than one student in more than one class. You may be totally unaware of how much you use certain words.

2. Use the **Signature Phrase Inventory** form on page 220. In the first column, list the verbal habits that are mentioned to you most often.

4. Read your list. For each verbal pattern, note the situation in which you use the word, phrase, or sentence. If you are not sure, ask students to help with this column.

3. Next, consider the future of each of these in your verbal repertoire. In the last column, note K, L, or A to indicate your plans to keep (and keep using well), lose (get rid of altogether), or adapt the verbal pattern.

4. Finally, create an action plan for any on the list that you will adapt. (Write this on the back of the form.) Will you experiment with different delivery tones? Will you emphasize certain words? Will you add a gesture to the phrase (such as my pretend seatbelt buckle movements when I call out "Buckle up!")? You may want to

experiment with different delivery tones. How about emphasizing certain words or syllables? Will you speak this word or phrase with a different accent? (This will wake them up!)

Own your words and phrases and have fun with them. It's your vernacular.

Action Step 6.5 Safe Humor

Pull together what you've learned about humor, and set some goals for using it to connect with your students.

1. Use the **Humor Dos & Don'ts** checklist on page 221. This checklist will help review ideas for using humor appropriately. In the left column, check items that you DO regularly. In the right column, check items that you regularly avoid. These are actions to which you are already committed.

2. Look at the items you have not checked. Circle any that you will add to your list of commitments to students about the use of humor. Use the back of the page to write at least five goals. Add a date for a re-check of these items.

3. Re-visit the list often, particularly to remind yourself to honor ALL the items in the right-hand column.

You've Gotta Connect

Action Step 6.6 Behold, the Class Clown!

This exercise gives you a chance to practice responses to some classic behaviors of class clowns.

1. Use the **Class Clown Scenarios** form on page 222. Three scenarios are described, each one fitting a category of class clown antics. Read the scenarios.

2. For each scenario, create a constructive response to give to the fictitious student—something that will affirm the student while managing his or her inclination to make similar comments in the future.

3. Next, create a brief action plan for communicating with the student in the future. How will you let the student know that the sense of humor is valued, at the same time you urge him or her toward its appropriate use?

Action Step 6.7 Managing the Class Clown

Here's a well-worn joke: A tourist visiting New York asked a native how to get to Carnegie Hall. The New Yorker's response, "Practice, practice, practice!" Any student teacher will tell you that the same is true in class management. If you want to get better at dealing with class clowns, you have to work at it. My high school speech teacher conducted "heckle day" once each year. On that day, students had the teacher's blessing to agitate the speaker with the goal of rattling her or him. It was fun to heckle. (It was not much fun to be on the

receiving end, but the teacher allowed no abusive talk.) We all performed both tasks. It was interesting that in our next round of speeches, everyone was calmer and more confident.

1. This action step is similar to "heckle day." If you are part of a group that is working through this book together, you have a ready group to help out. If you are reading this book alone, find a few heckling friends to donate some time to your growth.

2. Choose one of the scenarios from Action Step 6.6. With a partner, role play the scenario. This time, go beyond the teacher response that you wrote for Action Step 6.6. Each role-play should include—
   A. The scenario: The student detours the education process. The teacher responds. The student responds. You and your partner create a dialogue with the student answering back as a class clown might. You get to practice responding to each student comment.
   B. The affirmation: The teacher builds a relationship after the reprimand.

3. After the role-play, ask other members of the group to critique the performance. They can respond to prompts such as:

   • *How realistic was the role-play?*

   • *Describe the teacher's demeanor. Did they keep their cool?*

   • *Do you think the teacher's interventions would work? Explain.*

   • *Did the teacher seem genuine in their affirmations?*

You've Gotta Connect

JOKE REFLECTION

I told a joke about

_____

1 How did it feel to tell this to your students?

2 How did you feel about the joke? (Did you make the right choice? Was it the right length? Was it appropriate? Did they get it?)

3 Did students laugh?

4 What kind of feedback did you get from students that day or the next?

5 Could you see yourself telling more jokes? Why, or why not?

6 What adaptations will you make when you use jokes in the future?

ST🌀RY R🌀FL🌀CTI🌀N

Let me tell you!

I told a story about

---

1 How did it feel to tell this to your students?

2 How did the audience respond as you were telling the story?

3 What kind of feedback did you get immediately afterward?

4 What kind of feedback did you get the next day?

5 How did you feel about your delivery? (Was it the right length? Were you animated? Did you enjoy it?)

6 Could you see sharing more experiences in the future? Will you adapt aspects of your presentation?

You've Gotta Connect

Reproduce this page at 120% for 8½ x 11 size.

Signature Phrase Inventory

Now! Not next year!

Trust me, this is gonna be dynamite!

You coulda fooled me!

I betcha!

Words, Phrases, or Sentences I Use a Lot	When I Use This	Keep (K) Lose (L) Adapt (A)

Yes! You CAN!

I know this may seem pointless, but . . .

Awesome!

You're a genius!

HUMOR DOS & DON'TS

I DO

__ build a collection of humorous

jokes	tongue twisters
puns	silly sayings
quips	news stories
cartoons	headlines
stories	word play
riddles	comic strips

__ use these regularly in class

__ laugh at myself (in front of my students)

__ laugh WITH my students

__ welcome humor from students

__ add puns, quips, or cartoons to handouts and visual presentations

__ add fun or wacky decorations to the room

__ share short, fun, appropriate personal stories

__ occasionally show a funny video clip

__ laugh and smile a lot in my class

__ bring fun things or wear fun things

__ create fun quiz and test items

__ periodically break into song, poetry, or dance

__ regularly weave humor into lessons

__ watch closely to see how humor affects my students

I DON'T

__ joke about or poke fun at ethnicity or nationality

__ joke about or poke fun at religion

__ joke about sex or sexual orientation

__ joke about or poke fun at bodies, weight, or body types

__ use humor that in any way stereotypes or denigrates either gender

__ joke about or poke fun at disabilities

__ joke about death

__ poke fun at any student or group of students

__ use sarcasm

__ use any passive-aggressive humor

__ use any humorous put-downs

__ use humor to denigrate other staff members or parents

__ take part in inside jokes that do not include the whole group

__ ignore, tolerate, laugh at, join in on, or condone any of the above in my classroom or elsewhere in the school

__ continue or repeat any humor that makes one or more students uncomfortable

You've Gotta Connect

Reproduce this page at 120% for 8½ x 11 size.

Class Clown Scenarios

1. General Disruption

A student in Geometry class keeps making lame puns:

"This class is easy as pi!"

"This subject is for squares!"

"I just can't get the angle on this problem!"

"You keep falling right into my trapezoids!"

Create a response that affirms the student but establishes boundaries:	Create an action plan to affirm the student in future interactions:

2. Sarcasm

You're ready to begin a new novel in Literature class. One clown makes one sarcastic comment after another:

"We all saw the movie! We don't want to be les miserables for 900 pages!"

"This book is a great cure for insomnia!"

"Like this class of spoiled rich kids could ever relate to this book!"

Create a response that affirms the student but establishes boundaries:	Create an action plan to affirm the student in future interactions:

3. Derision

While your class works on an art project, one student can't stop the comments:

"Don't put Sam in my group; he draws like a preschooler!"

"Oh great, Olivia is in my group. All she talks about is her boyfriend!"

"Do you think we are actually going to do art projects for a living?"

Create a response that affirms the student but establishes boundaries:	Create an action plan to affirm the student in future interactions:

Learning Targets Checklist

To summarize what you have learned in this chapter,
check ✓ if you . . .

_____ can state five or more ideas about how humor deepens
connections with students.

_____ can describe several ways you welcome and include
humor in classroom life.

_____ can show that you have examined your use of humor in
the classroom.

_____ can summarize one joke and one story about your
personal life that you have told to students.

_____ can name several distinctions between appropriate and
inappropriate use of humor in the classroom.

_____ are able to share some ideas about life with classroom
clowns.

_____ are ready to name several ways you find joy with your
students.

_____ can verify that you have completed most of the Get-
Connected Action Steps in this chapter.

You've Gotta Connect

Chapter 7

Advocacy

Run Toward Trouble

Our school's resident intimidator rounded the corner and stomped down my hallway. I didn't know him personally. I did remember reprimanding him in the cafeteria for something—probably for being a jerk to someone. I recalled his confrontational response. After that, he was on my radar. I observed frequent, aggressive behavior toward staff members and other students. From what I could see, he was not a nice person; but some part of me wanted to connect with this kid.

I knew he was really struggling in a colleague's class. It surprised even me to hear my voice telling the principal, "I'd like a chance at reaching him. Transfer him to my class. I'm good with kids like him."

So he came scowling and challenging. He paused in front of my door, and within seconds the show began. He complained loudly about being moved. He complained that he always got blamed for everything. Then came the profanity. It was quite a scene. Thankfully, I maintained my cool. Between rants (when he had to take a breath), I told him to report to the office. He stared me down, shook his head, turned, and just walked away—certainly not in the direction of the office.

The next day, I sat in the office with the young man, the principal, and the resource officer. We three adults made it clear that he was running out of chances. He sat stoically. Did our warnings have any impact? It was anyone's guess.

The next few months involved a slow, painful process; but there was progress. By the end of the year, we were cordial. The next year when I didn't have him in class, he often sought me out to say "Hello" and tell me he missed me.

Maybe in the previous year when he was struggling so much, he only needed a change of venue. Or it could be that he was just comfortable with my personality. Perhaps he was on the verge of maturing, and my class happened to coincide with this growth. Regardless, I'm glad I reached out.

I can't say there was any magical transformation. He didn't become a National Honor Society member or win a Good Citizen of the School Award. He kept up his "jerkish" behavior in the hall and still got into a lot of trouble. But he had success in my class, whereas he'd experienced no success before the transfer.

Shortly before he graduated, we had one last interaction. I was doing lunch duty next to the office. He came stomping down the hall (obviously heading for a forced visit with the assistant principal) swearing like a Marine at Iwo Jima. After a particularly loud "f-bomb," he saw me, frowned, and nodded. "Sorry, Mr. Sturtevant," he said. Then, resuming his hostile attitude, he marched into the office. (I smiled, thinking maybe he had grown more than I realized.)

This is one example of a lesson I have learned many times: Stick out your neck for a kid, and you'll build a connection. Having that connection gives you a chance to influence that young woman or young man in some positive directions.

The Pitch 📢

You connect with students by being their advocate—sticking with them and standing up for them in times of trouble. I'm going to go further and say that troubled times are the best times for connection. A student who watches you go to bat for her will feel connected to you. A student who receives warmth and respect, even after swearing at you, will get a message of acceptance. A student who falls apart for some reason not even related to school and finds some compassion from you, will feel you are worth his trust. A student who fails a test or a whole quarter and gets support rather than disgusted lectures from you will believe that you are on her side.

Everything you have learned about connection, showing acceptance, affirming students, holding them to expectations, sharing yourself, enjoying your students, and being human comes together here. All the self-reflection and lessons learned serve you best when you run into a difficult student or a student with difficulties.

Just when you may want to run the other way, I urge you to stay and step toward kids in trouble. I urge you to gather with colleagues and parents in relationships that help kids when they need it. For this chapter on **advocacy**, your learning targets are:

Learning Targets

1. Embrace opportunities to approach conflicts or difficulties with connection.

2. Evaluate the ways you have responded to problems in the past.

3. Avoid reading trouble into situations.

4. Avoid making trouble where there really isn't any.

5. Examine your patterns for relating to different types of students.

5. Prepare or fine-tune a plan for assisting students who need intervention.

6. Take steps to confront conflicts and deepen connections with colleagues.

Look for Trouble

Armed with the belief that troublesome situations give you the absolute best opportunities for connection—be on the lookout for difficult times, blowups, setbacks, failures, hurt, and disappointments. This chapter is about troubleshooting. Troubleshooters are not just characters who survive tough or unpleasant situations. They are folks who act. They step into the troubled area. They use innovation and courage to work on solutions. You've read this book. You've made it through all the action steps (and even more bravely, through all my stories)! This puts you in the Troubleshooters Vanguard. I started this section with the word "armed." By now, you are armed with more than a belief. You are armed with a collection of understandings, attitudes, and strategies to take action. You know something about connecting. Now you can use that to help struggling students.

I'm looking for trouble. Have you seen any?"

What does it mean to "look for trouble"? It's a call to be aware of kids in need. Here are a few examples. It might be a student who

- is slipping academically

- looks withdrawn

- has a generally hostile attitude

You've Gotta Connect

- defies you, swears at you, or makes obscene gestures
- does poorly on a test
- has missed many classes or days of school
- hasn't turned in homework, again
- seems to be having a bad day
- is obviously struggling with an academic situation
- is obviously struggling with another teacher
- is isolated from other students
- has a broken heart
- is the object of gossip or whisperings
- steps on your ego
- has fallen out of connection with you
- is grumpy or belligerent
- is not the "kind" of kid with whom you easily connect
- has been dealt some bad cards (home difficulty, illness, poverty)
- gets in trouble in the hall or other place with a mass audience
- gets kicked off a sports team
- is obnoxious
- does just about anything to get attention
- is unpopular
- is backed into a corner by peers—literally or figuratively
- shows some sign of being bullied
- has hurt feelings
- is "in" or "out" of a clique
- has messed up

- has had a huge disappointment—social, academic, or otherwise

- has to work outside of school

- treats another student badly

- has been suspended or is about to be

A troublesome situation for a student can mean she is "in trouble" with you or another teacher. It can mean he has some difficulty with another student or a group of students. It can mean she has issues, setbacks, or disappointments that have little to do with you or any teacher. The trouble may be temporary or long lasting. Whatever the trouble is, it's a chance to connect.

I am not advising you to get into the middle of places where you do not belong. I don't advise you to conduct random interventions for kids outside of your class or to step on the toes of other educators in the school. (Never undermine a colleague's relationship with or decisions about one of her or his students.) This chapter is not an attempt to turn you into a counselor or the school's Dean of Behavior, or make you feel you are the answer to every student's problems. It is a call to watch for moments when there are natural, appropriate reasons and ways to reach out.

A connection with a kid in need is not a substitute for holding someone responsible for behavior. If the need involves an offense, the student must be held to the pre-explained consequences. In many situations, there are no consequences involved. But when there are, the connection comes during and after the follow-through on expectations.

Sometimes the guidance counselor or other teacher tells me that a student who's enrolled in my class has a reputation of being "a handful." I love this! It lights a passion about making a connection with that kid. Another ready-made scenario for connection plays out

> ### Listen to Students
>
> *Teachers who yell all the time don't connect well to students.*

regularly in the hall between classes. It's that scene where I have to confront a student. The majority of these are with kids who are not in my class. Somebody will shout the "F-word" or a young couple will be on the verge of an "R-rating" in the locker area. To me, the worst situations are when students verbally assault or physically intimidate one another. I have no problem confronting students in these circumstances because such behaviors are totally unacceptable.

Their response to me is predictable. If offenders know me, they usually comply and go on their way. If they don't know me, they might give me a lot of grief. I can be pretty blunt and direct when challenged, but I always make a mental note of the student and the situation. I look for an opportunity to build a different type of relationship when I have a chance. I often find myself hoping that the student will enroll in one of my classes. This scenario has played out many times, and it usually results in the beginning of a relationship.

In the future, I hope you'll thrive in such situations and view them as great opportunities. The ability to build relationships with kids others describe as "handfuls" will be one of your proudest accomplishments. **Do** appreciate the power of reaching out to a troubled kid! When you do, you give that kid a fighting chance!

Try **Get-Connected Action Steps 7.1 and 7.2.**, found later in this chapter. They will help you reflect on ways you have handled problems and conflicts in the past, and on how your actions affected relationships with students.

Don't Borrow Trouble

I love this old adage! It surely has a place in schools. There are plenty of difficulties already. Don't make something into a problem when it's not. Successful troubleshooters are open-minded. This means they are not tied to past patterns, reputations (theirs or the students'), rumors, successes, or failures. This also means that they are able to welcome new kids and new approaches.

I'll expand on some of the ways you as a teacher can borrow trouble—with hopes that you'll avoid them. **Don't**

- make assumptions about certain students based on their past reputations

- expect your students to have the judgment of wise adults

- let yourself get typecast as a certain kind of teacher who fits best with certain kinds of students

- assume that all students should like you or even warm up to you

- assume that, if a student isn't like you or doesn't like you, you won't bond with her or him

- take yourself too seriously

- take personally anything students say or do

- let the generation gap swallow you up

Listen to Students

The most disconnecting thing a teacher does is to have favorite students. This makes the others feel inadequate.

Here are six more topics with my advice about troublesome patterns that cause trouble where there really isn't any trouble.

Preconceived Notions

For so many students, the fallout from their previous behavior, accomplishments, or lack of accomplishment precedes them wherever they go. Others can't get a break from the cloud or halo of their siblings' reputations.

Forming ideas about a kid before you even meet him or her will create trouble that you don't need. Quite plainly, this is because you will have cheated yourself out of the chance to make your own assessments and build a relationship from a neutral stance. Trouble also follows from the fact that the student will not have a chance to make a fresh start or claim his or her own identity.

Author's Reflection

I remember the first staff meeting after I'd transferred to a new school. I was introduced to the staff. That was awkward. It grew more awkward when I sat down self-consciously amidst 60 pairs of evaluating eyes. During a lull in the meeting, others chatted about summer activities. Not knowing anyone, I looked through my paperwork. Out of habit, I gravitated to the class lists. My only exposure to the students at my new school had been coaching football for one month. I knew my freshman players and some of the varsity kids. I searched for them but could only find a few. The rest of the names were a vast pool of unknown persons.

Some of my more experienced colleagues seated around me noticed my focus and asked if they could see my list. I heard a lot of statements such as "Oh, you will like her" and "He is a great kid." Then, to my surprise, one teacher took out a pen and started to put checks on my list. The checks were like black marks from Santa. Each check was punctuated with a verbal warning such as, "You better watch out for this one" or "If he is anything like his brother, you are going to have your hands full!"

I was not a rookie teacher. I was, however, new to the school. I guess I didn't mind the heads up. I assumed she was just trying to help, but the warnings were creepy. The checkmarks were not erasable. Now that I look back, I see that it was a rude, obnoxious act. But it inspired my determination to have experiences with these kids that proved her predictions wrong.

The episode bothered me because I didn't ask for her input, and I was worried about being biased against those kids. It put me in a bunker mentality about kids I had not met. When I met them, I was leery. While I treated the "marked" students respectfully, there was a hesitation on my part. Many had significant issues. A cadre of vocal teachers found them confrontational. I was intent on forging a bond with each of them. Nevertheless, I did feel a draw into that vortex of pre-judging those students. I had to work hard to keep from getting sucked in completely. Be hyper-vigilant about this tendency. Don't sabotage potential connections by getting caught up in a siege mentality. Stay out of the bunker!

Unrealistic Expectations

When we expect that our students should always make rational choices, we've got problems. It amazes me how many teachers hold this belief! At least I know plenty who operate as if they do. They have all kinds of grief in classrooms and hallways because kids act like kids. Admittedly, I must count myself in this "they" group, at least some of the time. I fight this, often successfully. But I still have to work at it.

Think about your choices in life. Have you always made rational decisions? Not so for me. There are times when I ate too much, partied too much, didn't work hard enough, got into petty spats, gossiped too much, and made ridiculous decisions in relationships. I will wager that you have had similar experiences. And yet, when young people make boneheaded choices, we are just shocked, dumbfounded, and astounded! Here are some common statements from teachers about students and their choices:

- *Why is she attracted to him? Doesn't she know he will treat her badly?*
- *I can't believe he uses drugs!*
- *How is she going to get a good job if she doesn't apply herself?*
- *I don't think he realizes that the choices he is making have long-range implications!*
- *I am just trying to help her, and she treats me like an enemy!*
- *It is like he doesn't care about anything!*

You've Gotta Connect

When it comes to making poor choices, teens and preteens do not have the market cornered. Responsible, intelligent adults make absurd choices regularly. They have no intention of being unfaithful to their spouses, and yet they have affairs. They have too much to drink, and they drive home. They smoke cigarettes because they can't quit. They lie out in the sun for the temporary tan and ignore the aging effect on their skin. They eat unhealthy foods even though they have health problems. They injure people through gossip and look petty in the process. Got the picture? In each instance, adults with good intentions fall into the "poor choices" trap. They can't control their emotions or their appetites.

Cut your students some slack. If you try to hold them to unreasonable expectations, they'll fail. You'll be chronically disappointed, or worse, terminally disgusted. They'll feel misunderstood and disconnected.

Managing your expectations does not equate to dropping expectations. It doesn't mean that you ignore consequences. Set reasonable expectations. Hold students to reasonable consequences. At the same time, remind yourself frequently that students, like many adults, sometimes make the most asinine choices. Should you be frustrated? Certainly. But devastated? Never! Adapt and move on.

Reputations & Stereotypes

Child movie stars or other performers get put in a box. Early on, they are typecast. It's the same for teachers. Once you cultivate an image, it is exceedingly difficult to alter student perceptions. It's like never making a good first impression twice, and maybe worse. Each year that your image stays intact, it becomes more set in stone. And whatever role students (or other staff members) describe you as playing, the description travels from class to class, from year to year—all over the school (even the town).

This book is about connecting to *all* of your students. That is your mission. The name of the game is *diverse appeal*—connecting across the entire attitudinal spectrum. The last thing you want is to become "the jock teacher" who has no use for the non-athletes or the "the drama teacher" who thinks all the jocks are morons. You don't want to be known as "the scatterbrained one" or "the pushover." You don't want to be known as the teacher who only likes cool kids or the teacher who clicks exclusively with nerds.

The typecasting danger also includes what students think you believe. Once you're labeled as "the teacher who doesn't believe in homework," or "the liberal one," or "the anti-religion teacher," or anything like that—you've got trouble. Be careful in expressing opinions. You probably have strong views about many issues, but it is best to remain neutral. Students will ask about your views. It is more important to encourage their critical thinking than to indoctrinate them into your worldview. Boy, is this a tall order for many teachers! If you find this hard, remember this: Your goal is to connect. It'll be hard to connect with a student who gets that you find his or her views (or his parents') distasteful.

Naturally, you have a personality all your own. You have to be you. Yes, you'll be drawn to some students more than others. Certain types will annoy you, bore you, or scare you. Be aware of those with whom you don't connect easily. Students will sense this. Unchecked, this rut or reputation into which you've settled can lead some students to feel excluded, undervalued, discounted, or judged. When students feel you are not wholly "with" them, all kinds of disruptions and problems can follow.

Combat the typecasting. It is your job to work at an open mind and open heart to all kinds of students. It's what students deserve. It's a must for making connections! Follow some of the ideas and action steps in Chapters 2, 3, and 4 to show acceptance to kids with whom it does not flow easily. Also follow **Get-Connected Action Step 7.3**

You've Gotta Connect

later in this chapter to zero in on how students may typecast you and what you might do about it.

Differences & Disappointments

Not every student is going to be crazy about you. Get used to it. Get over it. Your behaviors and attitudes toward a student and your efforts to connect should not be dependent on how much the student likes you. Just as you don't gravitate naturally toward every student, so they won't all be drawn to you. Different kids naturally are attracted to different kinds of teachers. Expect this.

Ask Yourself:

How do I deal with people who don't like me?

Author's Reflection

Many years ago, I developed a great relationship with a student in my class. He was a riot, and I just loved being around him. The feeling was mutual. When we run into each other around the community now, we spontaneously disintegrate into laughter and enjoy reminiscing.

A few years after he graduated, his sister arrived in my class. I had no idea they were related, as the last name was a common one. What I did know was that this girl did not seem to like me. She was always scowling at me. I would tell an awesome story or make a hilarious comment and—nothing! In fact her eyes would seem to narrow in an aggressive way.

I made a mental note that I was going to develop a connection with this girl. My intent was to slowly work my way in without embarrassing or pressuring her. "I am going to wear her down," I thought.

Every time I saw her in the hall, I would smile and say, "Hello." Sometimes she would stare daggers, but mostly she would acknowledge me stiffly. In class, I would find reasons to compliment her. Though she used no inappropriate gestures of language, she would roll her eyes or sigh. The other kids in the class started to chide her: "Mr. S is so nice to you, and all you do is crab at him!"

I kept up the connection attempts. I figured it was a matter of time. The breakthough came one dreary Monday morning. She was at her desk yakking with her neighbors about her weekend when she mentioned her brother. I overheard the conversation. "Wait a minute!" I gasped. "Do you mean that so and so is your brother?" I continued, "He loves me!"

"Yes, I know. He talks about you all the time!" she responded in a bored, sarcastic tone.

Then I played my hand. "Well you and I have a strong relationship too, only ours is of the love-hate variety. I love you and you hate me!" She and everyone else in the room burst into laughter. Her heart melted and from then on we were cordial. She even initiated a "Hello" in the hall.

Many will read this story and think, "There is no way I would have put up with that kind of behavior for that long." Understood. When I was younger I wouldn't have either, but I have evolved. My self-worth is not bound up in whether a 16-year-old girl approves of me. My friendly demeanor toward her also demonstrated to my other students how to deal with difficult people. I am really proud of the way I handled this situation. It was a massive teachable moment and everyone benefited.

I want people to like me. (I despise the caveat "I don't care what other people think!" I have heard that statement from hundreds of adults and teenagers. In most cases, I believe it is usually bogus. Very few people truly don't care.)

In the span of a teaching career, you'll encounter thousands of students. Guess what? Some are not going to like you. Many will disappoint you. My little story about the former young lady is a tale of success, but it doesn't always work out that way. You are just going to repel some students. It may be something totally out of your control. I have some incredibly annoying traits. I accept that I am not everyone's cup of tea. It is utterly shocking that someone would not find me awesome, but it is a painful reality I have learned to accept. Embrace all students regardless of whether or not you are their favorite. If they sense your pullback because of less-than-adoring vibes they give, you'll be on the road to new troubles and poor connection.

Egos & Humility

If you decide to become a teacher, be prepared for brutal honesty. Adults don't always shoot straight, but your students will. If you've wondered whether your outfit matches or your haircut looks nice, you will soon learn the truth. That truth sometimes hurts.

I started to lose my hair young. When I was in my late 20's, students informed me on numerous occasions that my hair was exiting. By my 30's I said, "the heck with it" and shaved it off. Great decision. In a way, the whole situation helped me embrace my condition. Anyone balding goes through at least some denial. Thanks to my students, I was forced to accept my genetics. I knew that any teacher daring to sport a comb-over would last five seconds in a high school classroom. I'm a person of action, so out came the razor.

Student honesty extends to the non-physical realm. Be prepared for some blowback when you share your stories. You might get a few negative responses such as "This is stupid!" or "What does this have to do with anything?" Don't let such comments throw you off your game. Continue your connecting efforts.

Kids can also be harsh in evaluations of their teachers. You could be in the middle of your lesson when some cantankerous teen says, "Ms. X does a lot better job of teaching this!" On the other hand, those same critics can be wonderfully complimentary: "Mr. Z, you help me get math like no teacher ever has!" Kids rarely give false compliments. If you start hearing a lot of praise, you've hit the sweet spot.

So how do you deal with all this honesty? The key is your precious ego. Cultivate a healthy one, then strive to treat ego-bruising statements as opportunities. Accept that negative comments wound, see if you can learn anything from them (you can learn a lot more from criticism than praise), and then let them go. It is not an easy practice, but it is a worthy endeavor.

Keep in mind that young people think out loud. Keep in mind that pre-adolescents and adolescents can be pretty obnoxious. Most of the time, their purpose is not to hurt you. They are just blabbing. (I'm sure you can tell the difference between honest comments and intentional insults.)

Yes, this is perhaps overused advice, but hear it nonetheless: **Don't take students' comments personally.** And for sure, don't turn every honest comment into a confrontation. Don't make something a problem because it scrapes your ego. As you develop your ability to handle negative comments, you might just be pleasantly surprised to find that they dwindle in frequency. Some students just want to get a rise out of you. When they see that you don't take the bait, they'll get bored.

When it comes to corralling the ego, be ready to laugh at yourself. So many teachers take themselves too seriously. This stirs up trouble and makes problems where problems don't exist. Throw in some self-deprecating humor now and then. Take embarrassments in stride. (If you teach middle or high school, it is oh, so easy to embarrass yourself in front of your students.) If you can laugh at yourself after you say something dumb, trip over your feet, choke on your pencil, misstate a word so it comes out as a swear word, or inadvertently make some uncouth body noises—you'll go a long way toward connecting with students. You'll also avoid borrowing trouble.

Connections Over the Long Haul

As I said earlier in the book, here is just one of the bizarre things about education: You age but your students don't. My first year of teaching, I was not much older than my students. It was a tough position for a young teacher, because I identified a lot more with my students than my colleagues. (Fortunately, I knew enough not to socialize with the students. If you are a young teacher, DON'T FALL INTO THIS TRAP, it is a career killer!)

? Foiled again?

But Mr. Sturtevant, we already watched that movie today on our cell phones.

In April of that year, a girl in my class piped up, "Mr. Sturtevant, I saw a movie with my boyfriend this weekend that you must go see. It's called *The Breakfast Club*. This actor Emilio Estevez looks just like you!" Others chimed in their agreement. That was a movie that I had to see! Keep in mind, this was back when I had hair. I went to see it, and by gosh—I did look like Emilio Estevez. I was really flattered. I returned to class and shared my enthusiasm.

Feeling pretty full of myself, I went to the teacher's lounge and told everyone present (all of them over 40) about the incident. They looked at me strangely. A crusty older male teacher asked, "Who the heck is Emilio Estevez?" (He didn't say "heck." He used another word.) That seals it, I thought; I have nothing in common with these people!

The incident came full circle this past school year. One day when my students were talking about how a staff member resembled a certain actress, I could not resist telling my story about Emilio Estevez. Almost in unison the students responded, "Who is Emilio Estevez?" *C'est la vie.*

Connecting over the long haul is no easy task. When you are younger, you have similar generational references. You are a bit like their older siblings. Things change quickly. After a few years you become like a cool older cousin; then you transition into the hip younger uncle or aunt. Unfortunately, you then morph into their parents, and if you stay long enough, you are older than their parents and border on *granparent-dom*!

Young teachers, don't panic. This doesn't happen overnight, but it does happen. Maintaining your ability to connect is simple: Accept each generation of students. There is nothing new about generation gaps. Be yourself, but allow the younger generation members to express themselves. A quick way to sever connections is to point out to today's youth that they are somehow weird, deficient, inferior, or screwed up.

Handle Double Trouble

In any school, particularly middle and high schools, you can be sure many troubles will surface. You can't have a big group of kids and adults living together for many hours a day without this. There are some kids, however, for whom troubles are deeper, more persistent, or more numerous. They need more than the usual approach of confident teachers using stated guidelines and expectations supported

You've Gotta Connect

by clear, consistent application of outlined consequences. They need interventions beyond this approach. I want to share a personal evolution that has helped me deal with these kids more effectively.

About 10 years ago, an administrator asked me to join him and some other school staff and community members in a training project designed to help kids in trouble. We pulled together an intervention assistance team and went off to train in the *Masonic Model Student Assist Program*. I am not a committee guy. My experience with meetings and committees is that there is a whole lot of yakking and not much doing. But when our little delegation attended the Masonic training a few weeks later, I was impressed. Recently, our school embraced the *Response to Intervention* program (RTI). I've watched both these programs provide real, lasting help for students, and I hope every school has or begins an assistance team for students.

My participation on the student assistance team was one of the best experiences in my professional career. In the process of helping troubled students evolve socially and academically, I noticed a fundamental improvement in my ability to connect with such kids. In turn these bonds were even greater catalysts for students' growth. My experience on the team also gave me a *can-do* spirit. I began to enjoy the challenge of building connections with distant and troubled kids. I grew; students benefited—what a great combination of outcomes!

I began to use a similar systematic approach to identifying problems and designing interventions with the struggling students in Room 111 (my classroom). I'll share the steps I follow for intervention for a student. You can see a flowchart summary of my plan for student assistance below. Here, I'll elaborate on each of those steps.

Ask Yourself:

Who reached out to you when you were young?

Student Assistance Plan

A Flowchart for Intervention

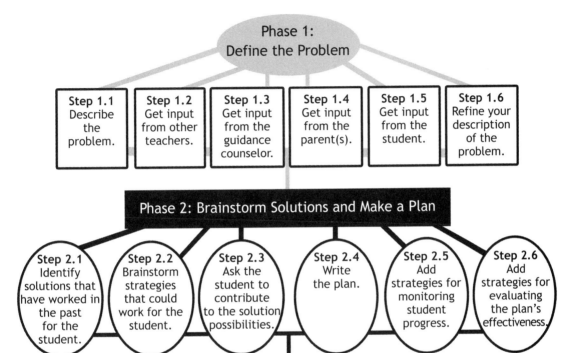

Phase 1: Define the Problem

Step 1.1 Describe the problem.

Step 1.2 Get input from other teachers.

Step 1.3 Get input from the guidance counselor.

Step 1.4 Get input from the parent(s).

Step 1.5 Get input from the student.

Step 1.6 Refine your description of the problem.

Phase 2: Brainstorm Solutions and Make a Plan

Step 2.1 Identify solutions that have worked in the past for the student.

Step 2.2 Brainstorm strategies that could work for the student.

Step 2.3 Ask the student to contribute to the solution possibilities.

Step 2.4 Write the plan.

Step 2.5 Add strategies for monitoring student progress.

Step 2.6 Add strategies for evaluating the plan's effectiveness.

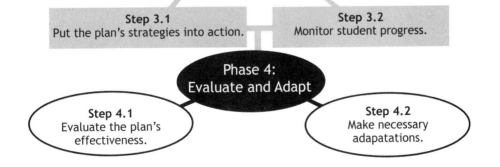

Phase 3: Implement the Plan

Step 3.1 Put the plan's strategies into action.

Step 3.2 Monitor student progress.

Phase 4: Evaluate and Adapt

Step 4.1 Evaluate the plan's effectiveness.

Step 4.2 Make necessary adapatations.

You've Gotta Connect

Phase 1: Define the Problem

Step 1.1 Describe the problem. *In a few sentences, state clearly what you believe the problem to be. Work on one problem at a time.*

Step 1.2 Solicit input from other teachers. *See if the student is experiencing similar problems with your colleagues. Notice any differences in the ways teachers experience this student.*

Step 1.3 Contact the guidance counselor *to learn whether he or she has any experience with this student.*

Step 1.4. Call the student's parent. *Make it your first priority to let the parent know you are on their side and the child's side and want to help their child. Many times the parent is overwhelmed by the kid's behavior. Parents must be reassured that you are **with** them on the same team. Be careful not to sound judgmental. Work hard to cultivate this relationship.*

Step 1.5 Interview the student. *Form a series of questions that you can ask any student who is experiencing hardship. With practice the questions will become second nature. With these questions ready, talk with the student. This is where you can start to build the foundations of a strong future relationship. As a part of this chat, find out*

- *how the student explains or defines the problem*
- *if the student accepts that there **is** an issue*
- *if the student is willing to receive help*
- *how he or she feels about the relationship with you*
- *if the student feels that you are is exacerbating the problem*

Be diligent in this commitment to learn from the student. This process may require that you develop a thick skin. You may be annoyed by what the student says. Try to listen more than you talk. Don't be defensive. Don't attempt to explain your tactics. This is not about you! This is a time to learn about the student.

Step 1.6 Refine your description of the problem. *Use the information you have gained from other sources, in combination with your own views, to restate the problem.*

Phase 2: Brainstorm Solutions and Make a Plan

Step 2.1 Identify solutions that have worked in the past for the student. *When you interview teachers, parents, and the student, be sure to ask about what has been tried in the past. Find out how those past interventions have worked. You may be fortunate to learn some techniques that have been effective. For any that have not worked, you'll be challenged to adapt them or drop them in favor of some novel approaches.*

Step 2.2 Brainstorm new strategies that could work for this student. *Gather approaches, goals, tasks, and techniques that you'll consider as part of an assistance plan.*

Step 2.3 Ask the student to contribute to the solution possibilities. *If the student is receptive to help, ask him or her to take part in creating an intervention plan. Ask questions such as*

> *· What would motivate you to change?*

> *· Which of these ideas would you choose for addressing this problem?*

> *· How can I help?*

Even if the student is not receptive, remember that your emphasis is on empowering the student. You can gather a list of possible steps and give the student some choices.

Step 2.4 Write the plan. *Write steps and strategies that you, other school staff members, the parents, or the student (or any combination of the above) will follow. Make sure it includes actions for teacher, student, and parents. Write tasks or expectations in clear terms that say what will happen. Keep to a reasonable*

You've Gotta Connect

number of steps. Choose steps that can actually be accomplished. For each one, identify who is involved and who is responsible for the implementation.

Step 2.5 Add strategies for monitoring student progress. *Develop a method to periodically record the student's progress or lack of progress. Include dates when you will check in on various strategies.*

Step 2.6 Add strategies for evaluating the plan's effectiveness. *Don't implement a plan until you have decided what the end goals are, what the student or others will do (with your help), and how you will tell when the student has succeeded or when the strategy is successfully completed. Set dates for evaluating each part of the plan.*

Phase 3: Implement the Plan

Step 3.1 Put the plan's strategies into action. *Once you have written down tactics or steps and specified who is responsible for each, it's easy to follow the narrative of the plan. Refer to the written plan frequently to keep focus on the tasks.*

Step 3.2 Monitor student progress. *Follow the student's progress and the completion of tasks as they are outlined. Keep a record of what happens. Don't be narrow-minded. While your goal may be specific and you may not see movement toward it, you could see growth in other areas. For example, you may want the student to complete more of her assignments and you don't see much evidence of this, but at the same time, you notice an improved relationship with her, that is growth! Don't overlook it. It is an open door and you should walk through and look for the next opportunity.*

Phase 4: Evaluate and Adapt

Step 4.1 Evaluate the plan's effectiveness. *Record your views about where the process has taken you both. Contemplate successes* *and failures. Be open and flexible. Look at what really happened. Notice things that happened that you did not expect. Don't be rigid about how success has to look. Too many times we have this mental script of the way everything is supposed to go. If we let go of the script and make reasonable adjustments, we can evolve along with the student.*

Include students in the evaluation. Get their feedback about how things worked. Have them identify successes and failures. Talk about what to do next. Call the student's parent. Let them know what happened. Let them know how you assess the progress. Talk about what to do next. Unless the problem is solved, begin the process anew.

Keep confidential information to yourself. Be careful about what you put in writing and where you keep it. Shred stuff that is no longer needed.

Complete the exercise in **Get-Connected Action Step 7.4** at the end of this chapter to examine the effectiveness of your past intervention efforts. Then move on to **Get-Connected Action Step 7.5** to design your own plan for assisting a student who needs intervention.

Too often, the kids with "double trouble" scare us away. The obstacles to helping them seem insurmountable. Their protective behaviors and attitudes intimidate us. Connecting with them seems impossible. Yes, there are barriers. But attach them with confidence. Better yet, attack them with enthusiasm. As your confidence grows, the obstacles will lose power. Once your paradigm shifts, you will be amazed at how your problems seem so much more manageable.

You've Gotta Connect

Confront Colleague Trouble

You need your colleagues. They need you. The best setting for students, especially students in trouble, is one wherein colleagues work in harmony to help students surmount problems.

Take care with your colleague connections. Not only are peaceable, cooperative, respectful (yes, and dare I say, enjoyable) relationships critical to helping kids in all aspects of their school lives, but your relationships with your colleagues also serve as models of connection for your students to watch and mimic. And don't ever be fooled. Though adolescent and preadolescent students are masterful at ignoring the adults around them, they do notice how you interact with each other.

Ask Yourself:

Do you ever feel you have more issues with colleagues than students?

Furthermore, your well-being (and thus your ability to be an effective teacher and connector to students) is tied up with your job satisfaction. It's hard to be content at work if you have ongoing conflicts with or disconnection from your colleagues. Take some steps to start enjoying more of your colleagues more often. You can even take a risk and ask a few to do something fun with you—choosing some with whom you do not usually associate. Challenge them to pass on the favor. Who knows? This effort could have positive ripple effects throughout the staff.

I'd have to write another book to address all the issues, wounds, delights, and strategies (not to mention the stories!) on the topic of building decent relationships among the adults who educate children. So I'll just plead: **"Know that learning to connect well with students is related to and influenced by your connections with colleagues."** Watch out for jealousies, petty behaviors, and fragile egos. Don't get into competitions about who is the better teacher (or who is better at connecting with kids). Don't get resentful if a colleague is better at something (such as connecting with kids) than you are. Don't break your arm patting yourself on the back for becoming proficient at connecting with kids. Don't be afraid to grow because you fear snide or jealous comments from colleagues. Support and nurture each other. Remember that when one of you wins, you all win. When you win together—the students win! That's the goal anyway.

Make sure you complete **Get-Connected Action Steps 7.6 and 7.7** later in this chapter. They will aid your efforts at building better connections with colleagues.

I'll end with a story. (Of course!)

Author's Reflection

Not long ago, our teacher's lounge went through a tectonic shift. Originally, it was a perfect metaphor for a middle school dance. All the women sat in the lounge chairs on one side, and the guys sat around a large circular table on the other. The room was as separated by conversation theme as by gender. The women tended to talk about their families, school issues, and students. The men, ensconced at the "round table," engaged in endless sports talk.

One day, seated on the side of the "round table" that put me in earshot of the "sorority," I could hear the women dishing. The volume and velocity of the talk was spiking. The majority of the females were talking simultaneously, gesturing wildly. I couldn't resist, I elbowed my good friend, pointed toward that side of the room, and said, "Check it out!" Before I knew it, the entire "round table" silently observed this verbal orgy. It took some time, but finally the women caught on. They stopped, stared us down, and demanded, "WHAT!?"

You've Gotta Connect

I spoke up, "Do you guys know how pissed off you sound every day at lunch?"

As you can imagine, my comment was not embraced. "At least we don't waste time blabbing about some stupid game! We talk about important things!" was the curt response.

The volleys came fast and furiously after that. It took some time to restore order, but soon we began to laugh together and question the segregated nature of our lounge.

The next day, some brave females waltzed in and plopped down at the "round table." We were shocked and impressed. We told them they were welcome, but that we were not going to talk about school or kids. They agreed, and we all enjoyed the conversation. Slowly our room became more integrated. The school-talk subsided, and the guys expanded their play list.

As it was late spring, the school year nearly over. While it lasted, it was wonderful. Lunch was fun! We would laugh to the point that someone stuck a head in the door and said the teachers could hear us in the hall. (We had to tone down because our talk was not always kept to a PG rating.) Our little lunch experiment left us refreshed and with a sense of camaraderie. Next year I am going to pull a Rosa Parks and sit on the female side.

Our schools are filled with troubled students. Bonding with them is the best way to help. Create a plan and gain the chutzpah to become a confident troubleshooter. As result of your efforts, relationships can be forged and troubled students can thrive. So buckle up, because one of your students' "check engine" light just came on!

Follow the action steps to grow as a troubleshooter. Then, don't neglect to finish the chapter by summarizing what you learned in the chapter. See the **Learning Targets Checklist** on the final page of Chapter 7.

Get-Connected! Action Steps

Action Step 7.1 How Did I Handle That?

Here's a chance to take a look at how you've handled some problems
in the past (recent or distant). Think about broken expectations,
students' mistreatment of one another, or any kind of trouble in the
classroom or elsewhere in the school. Think about problems with the
class as well as incidents that involve one, two, or a few students.
Identify four incidents.

1. Make a copy of the **Problems Revisited** form on
   page 258. Write a brief description of each of the
   four problems.

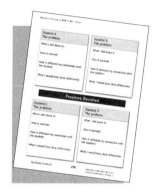

2. For each one, tell what you did or how you
   reacted.

3. Think about how your reaction affected your
   relationship with the student or group.

4. Now dig a little deeper. Was there anything you could have done
   differently? Think about this and write one different tactic you
   would try if you could go back to the incident.

Action Step 7.2 Welcome to Conflict!

If you have been teaching any length of time (like a week), you've
no doubt had some conflicts with students (defiance, anger, bad
language, disregarding of rules, and such). Take time to reflect on
one conflict—one that ended with no abatement of the behavior and

perhaps with heightened animosity. I have no trouble conjuring up past uncomfortable confrontations. I will wager that you have no trouble doing the same.

1. Make a copy of the **Anatomy of a Conflict** form on page 259.

2. Briefly describe the conflict. Do not use the student's name.

3. Briefly describe how you felt in the midst of this conflict.

4. Briefly describe your reaction—what you did.

5. Tell what happened. How did the situation end? How did your response affect the situation?

6. Now comes the hard part. Think about how you could have responded more effectively. Take some time. This will challenge you and help you. Similar situations will surface, and next time you will anticipate your emotions and be ready. If you need some help with this step, have the chutzpah to ask a peer familiar with the situation for some feedback. (Be prepared, and get some honest, critical feedback! Understand that you asked the question, and the peer is probably trying to help.)

Action Step 7.3 Typecasting the Teacher

It's time to analyze the image you've portrayed to students (i.e., your reputation or type). In this chapter, I've encouraged you to work hard to avoid getting pigeonholed into one "persona," to appeal to the broad spectrum of students, and to avoid ramming your personal views down your students' throats. Here's a chance to make some healthy moves away from having one label.

1. Make a copy of the **Break the Mold** form on page 260. Think about the things you've heard about yourself. Write a brief description of how students or others in the school typecast you. If you're having trouble with this, ask some students or colleagues for help.

2. Next, consider how this description of you is constructive and how it is limiting.

3. Then, choose three of the limitations you listed. For each one, write some things you might do differently to counteract that limitation.

You've Gotta Connect

Action Step 7.4 Past Efforts

In the pursuit of effective troubleshooting with students, it's helpful to examine interventions and measures you have tried in the past. Do this in preparation for Action Step 7.5 where you will outline your own plan for helping students solve a problem.

1. Identify an intervention that you used with a student. It could be one that worked well or one that did not.

2. Make a copy of the **Student Assistance Plan** flowchart on page 243. Circle any flowchart steps that you attempted in your intervention.

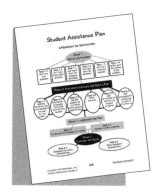

3. Near each circled step, write a comment about its effectiveness. This could relate to how you did the step, how it worked, the student's reaction, or anything that happened. Do not write the student's name on the page.

4. Highlight any of the steps you did complete that were especially difficult or contentious.

5. Put a star beside any steps you did not use but you now think might have helped.

6. On the back of the page, write a few sentences to describe the overall effectiveness or outcome of your intervention. What went well? What worked? What mistakes did you make during the intervention? What would you do differently? How did the student and/or parents respond?

7. If you are working through this action step with a group, share your reflections.

Action Step 7.5 Your Intervention Plan

Following your work in Action Step 7.4, you're ready to work on your own plan.

1. Go back to pages 241 through 247. Review the pictured summary of the **Student Assistance Plan** flowchart and the explanation of the steps. Consider what parts of that plan might work for you.

2. Remembering that the goal is to help students and build strong relationships with them in the process, plan your own flowchart.

3. Use the 2-page template **Plan for Student Assistance** on pages 261 and 262, or create your own template. You can label the process with stages, steps, activities, strategies, or whatever works for you. Write a summary version of your plans on these pages. Use as many ideas from the flowchart in this book as you want. But make it your own plan.

4. Then, go back and focus on the details. You'll probably need more paper.

5. Once you have completed your flowchart, present the summary to colleagues or other members of your study group. Listen to their feedback; then make adaptations in your plan.

You've Gotta Connect

Action Step 7.6 Turnaround: The Inside Story

Interaction with colleagues is a big deal! Many educators report that their biggest struggles are disputes with fellow teachers, not conflicts with the students. For this exercise, you'll focus on turning around a relationship that is troublesome. It might be a connection that already has taken a positive turnaround, or one that needs to turn around.

1. Think of a relationship that, at some point, caused you anxiety.

2. Make a copy of page 263, **The Turnaround**. In the first box, write a brief description of the relationship and why it caused or still causes anxiety.

3. Consider the signals you projected (or still project) that give connecting or disconnecting messages. Think about subtle things you may have broadcast. Temporarily suspend your ego and try to reflect on your interactions from the prospective of your antagonist. What might you have said or done that increased the tension or mistrust?

4. Move to the circle. Write some steps you took or things that happened to turn this anxiety-ridden relationship into a closer connection. If that has not happened, write some steps you **could** try, with the goal of making a turnaround.

5. In the last rectangle, describe how the relationship looks now (if there has been a turnaround). If there has not been a change for the better, describe how you wish or hope the relationship will look in the future.

Action Step 7.7   It's Not Just Lunch

Lunchtime is often the time when colleagues interact most. It is a prime opportunity for building friendly relationships with colleagues. This won't happen if you hide in your room or cluster up with the same few people every day. Take time to evaluate your daily lunch experience. Ask yourself the following questions. If you are working through this step with a group, share your answers honestly with one another.

- *Do I isolate myself at lunch?*
- *Have I developed any staff friendships through lunch?*
- *Is the atmosphere in our lunchroom or lunchtime positive or negative?*
- *Is our lunchroom segregated by gender?*
- *How do I respond when colleagues criticize students?*
- *What are the general topics of conversation?*
- *Do people get angry in our lunchroom?*
- *What would my ideal lunch with colleagues look like?*
- *What could I do to improve the atmosphere at lunchtime?*

At lunch you can learn, network, unwind, bond, and catch your breath. Learn to love lunch. Make it more than just lunch!

Student A
The problem:

What I did about it:

How it worked:

How it affected my connection with the student:

What I would have done differently:

Student B
The problem:

What I did about it:

How it worked:

How it affected my connection with the student:

What I would have done differently:

Problems Revisited

Student C
The problem:

What I did about it:

How it worked:

How it affected my connection with the student:

What I would have done differently:

Student D
The problem:

What I did about it:

How it worked:

How it affected my connection with the student:

What I would have done differently:

258

Anatomy of a Conflict

The Conflict

How I Felt About It

How I Reacted

The Effectiveness of My Reaction

How I Could Have Responded Differently

Reproduce this page at 120% for 8½ x 11 size.

BREAK THE MOLD

How I think my students typecast me:

(Mr., Mrs., Ms) _____
is the

Ways this view is constructive:

1. _____

2. _____

3. _____

4. _____

5. _____

Ways this view is limiting:

1. _____

2. _____

3. _____

4. _____

5. _____

Choose 3 limitations. Write three good ideas for mitigating the limitation.

1

Limitation:

1.

2.

3.

2

Limitation:

1.

2.

3.

3

Limitation:

1.

2.

3.

PLAN FOR STUDENT ASSISTANCE

A Flowchart for Intervention

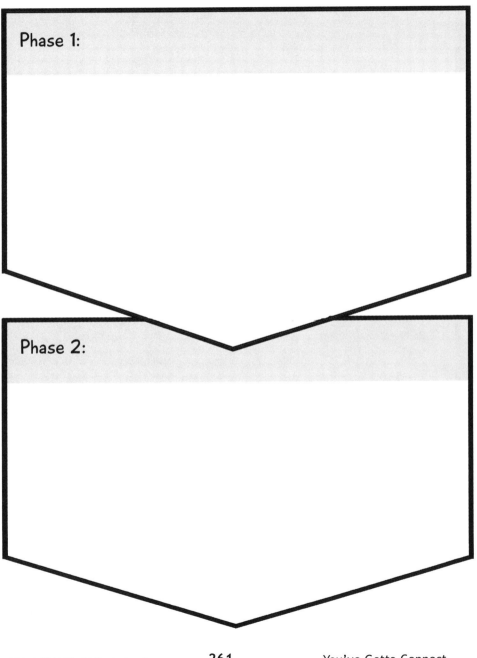

Phase 1:

Phase 2:

A Flowchart for Intervention, cont.

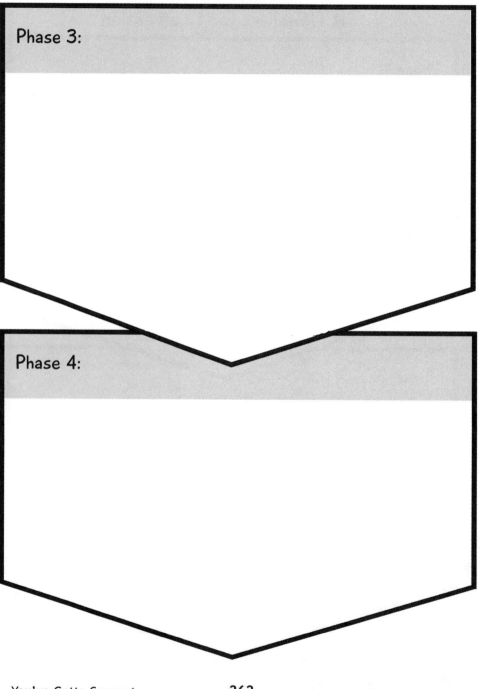

Phase 3:

Phase 4:

THE TURNAROUND

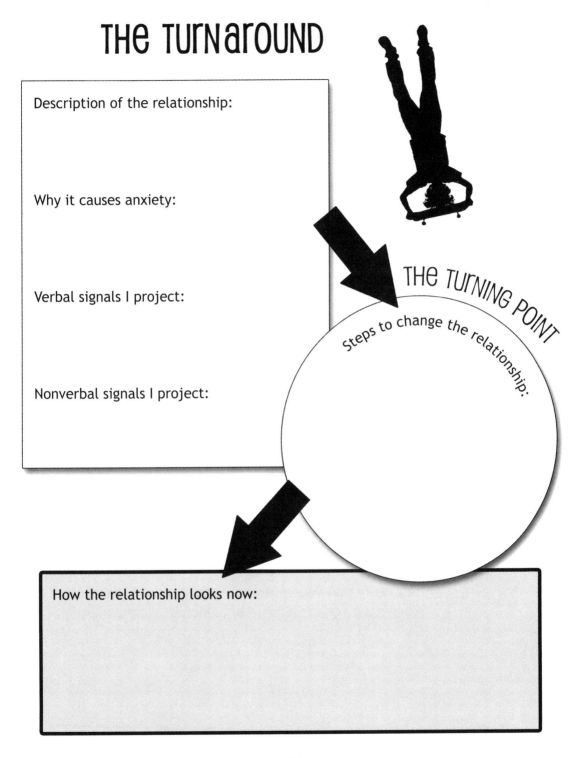

Description of the relationship:

Why it causes anxiety:

Verbal signals I project:

Nonverbal signals I project:

THE TURNING POINT

Steps to change the relationship:

How the relationship looks now:

Learning Targets Checklist

To summarize what you have learned in this chapter, check ✓ if you . . .

_____ have identified ways to look for troublesome situations that can lead to connection.

_____ can name several ways to avoid borrowing trouble by rethinking expectations, preconceived notions, stereotypes, students' preferences, and your ego.

_____ have evaluated the ways you have responded to some troublesome incidents and conflicts.

_____ assessed the way students or colleagues typecast you.

_____ have reflected upon your past approaches for intervention to assist students with difficulty.

_____ have drafted a plan for student intervention in your classroom.

_____ can describe two or more steps you will take or have taken to improve connections with colleagues.

_____ can verify that you have completed most of the Get-Connected Action Steps in this chapter.

Yes, there's more!

I felt that I was slipping. Perhaps I was getting too old for this game. One class caused me great anxiety. As a group, they were quite withdrawn. They didn't seem very interested in Economics, nor in my engaging stories or personality. I'd reached reluctant kids before--so why not this group? Was I losing my edge?

I worked hard—very hard, to win them over. I told my stories with more gusto and animation. I sought out individual students in the hallway and overextended myself. The returns on my efforts were marginal.

One night during that frustrating semester, I noticed a friend request on my Facebook page. Amazingly, a certain 35-year-old former student was requesting a digital relationship. I say it was amazing because this student had never given me the time of day. In fact, he had seemed hostile. Intrigued, I accepted his request. Over the course of some back-and-forth messages, I learned that he actually enjoyed my class and valued me as a mentor. I would never have guessed!

A past conversation with Carol Weiss, a local Presbyterian minister, came to mind, "Jim, teachers never know who they're impacting. The scowling kid with the folded arms might be precisely the student with whom you are connecting the most."

Her wise words finally registered. Perhaps I was trying too hard with my problem class. They weren't causing my anxiety. It was my problem, and I was probably passing it on to them. I reminded myself that I am a friendly person to whom reaching out comes naturally. I decided to temper my ego, quit forcing things, and just relax. It helped—a lot! Who knows? Perhaps I'll get some future Facebook requests from this crew.

The seven chapters you've read with all the action steps you've followed have offered plenty of ideas to fill your toolbox and heart. By now, you are deep into improving connections. I leave you with a few "after words" to keep in mind as you continue this journey.

Be Yourself

This advice is short and to the point. Earlier in the book, I talked about how kids can tell if you are real. Connecting with kids does take work. It wasn't a mistake for me to be eager about connecting with every class. It was mistake for me to let the plan—the idea—overshadow the human element. Don't lose sight of who you are naturally. Trying to be something you are not, or trying to force things will lead to failure. Follow the ideas in this book in your way. There's no connection if kids feel it's forced on them. Work at it, but be cool! Through it all, remain friendly, welcoming, and inquisitive.

Stay Alive

In the midst of my first year of teaching, I made a great friend. John Frye was the Physical Science instructor at my school and had five years experience, so he was my unofficial (and rather unorthodox) mentor. He was a fascinating guy who had lived and worked in a wide variety of fascinating jobs and locations, including a stint on an oil rig. A voracious reader, John seemed to know something about any topic that arose. One night when we were discussing life, the universe, and everything in it, he piped up: "Jimmy, in this job we are like rats in a cage. The bell rings and we run to this room. We do our little act for fifty minutes. Then the bell rings again and we run to the next class and do the same. In the middle of our day, we wolf down lunch, and then hustle through the afternoon. We do the same day after day year after year."

Whoa! This was not uplifting to a new teacher! I asked John why he stayed in teaching. He was adamant, "It is a great job, and I have tried others." He explained that he loved the work, but that the routine could be a struggle. I have thought about his statement a lot. While the routine nature of teaching is not a huge turnoff for me, I have had moments when I felt claustrophobic.

Ten years ago I represented our school in a program of partnership between schools and the private sector. I was the only educator. During the first meeting of the group, we were asked to tell about our typical day. As I listened to these stressed-out attorneys, managers, and accountants, I thought about the fun of being with young people, the many moments of enjoyment every day, the energy in a high school, the never-boring dynamics of my day, the endless variety of personalities, and the satisfaction of seeing human beings grow. I know that the job has routine. I know it has challenges and frustrations. But as I sat there waiting for my turn to speak, I thought, "My day sounds a lot better than theirs."

Recognize the *life* in your profession. Don't let yourself settle into mind-numbing routines. Even with all the rules, standards, state mandates, and protocols, you have plenty of control over the way your day goes. You can be creative and flexible with your teaching strategies. You can switch things up to keep class lively for yourself! And of course, if you get along with your students, there are surprises and pleasures that defy the routine!

The worst thing you can do is run on a rat wheel without making real efforts to hop off. If you stay in a deadly routine, you'll lose passion for your profession. Your students will read the signs. You'll be less effective as a communicator and connector to them. They'll be less attracted to a connection with you.

Like a rat on a wheel!

10:45

One hour until lunch. But hold on, is it Monday or Tuesday? Come to think of it, what year is it?

You've Gotta Connect

Grow

Teaching is a demanding profession. Nevertheless, some find it possible to be slackers. While most of us are motivated and perform at a high level without bonuses dangled in front of us, it takes planning and purpose to keep growing and improving.

There are lots of reasons to grow personally and professionally. Most of those have to do with benefits to your joy in life, your intellectual stimulation, your relationships with friends and families, and your job satisfaction. And of course, you want to do a better job of teaching what your students need to learn. But do you realize the big, positive effects your own growth has on your relationships with students? Yes! If young people see you learning or trying something new, they'll be much more interested in you and feel more drawn to you.

My summers have always been dedicated to personal growth. In the summers, I read, explore, experience, investigate, and push boundaries. My wife calls my little detours *jaunts* (probably because most of them are short-lived). But many of these excursions have added tremendously to my life and have made me a vastly more interesting person (in my opinion).

In the summer of 1993, I took one such detour and discovered a more scenic, inspiring route through life. A sports massage therapist suggested that I take up yoga. I thought it a strange recommendation, but being open-minded, I gave it a try. I borrowed some VHS tapes from the library, and on a quiet, cloudy, summer afternoon, I sprawled on my living room floor and assumed 4,000-year-old poses from the Asian subcontinent's distant past. (You young teachers may have to google "VHS" on the Internet to find out what VHS tapes are—or were.)

It felt awkward. I was pushing my body into positions that years of workouts restricted. Yet I felt a deep wisdom in the practice. My body, although protesting, was reluctantly approving. The *piece de resistance* was the meditation segment at the end of the tape. I experienced the humor and horror of a mind that could not keep still. The instructor on my videotape said, "Concentrate on your breathing." I could do this only briefly before my mind would take off in several directions at high velocity.

It was enlightening indeed. I had not been aware how closed my body was, and I'd had no idea my mind was so hyper. I began a regular practice of stretching. It was an activity that I could do anywhere for free. The only equipment required was my body and my mind. I improved. I became calmer. With work, I became moderately flexible and definitely more aware. My disposition benefited dramatically. I will do this practice for the rest of my life.

Becoming a yoga fan has had unintended consequences. Two years later, I was asked to teach ancient history. I introduced students to a brief history of yoga before we retired to the hall to practice some stretches. I was worried they wouldn't take it seriously; they did laugh a lot, but they eagerly did everything I asked. They loved it! Here a diverse group of students were all lying on the floor together experiencing something new. I even did a one-minute silent meditation at the end where they all sprawled quietly and relaxed. The subtle sounds of the building sprung to life, and many noticed them for the first time. At the end, their demeanors were calm and positive.

The next day, they all begged for more—even the students who had originally grumbled the most. It's become a staple of my class; I have stretched 15 years worth of students. I even started a morning stretch club. And you'd better believe, I have formed some strong bonds with the students who periodically stop by in the morning for a stretch!

You've Gotta Connect

Take Care of Yourself

The plane is ready for takeoff. The flight attendant goes through the routine of emergency instructions. She explains that oxygen masks will drop if the cabin loses pressure. You know the drill; if you travel by plane, you've heard it over and over. You are to put on your oxygen mask first, then assist others who may need help.

As teachers and parents, it's natural to rush to help out kids first. I'd have a terrible time in an emergency not protecting my tender offspring first. (Although now they are old enough that, hopefully, they would strap on their own masks and then rescue me.)

The airline people are right. You have to take care of yourself if you are going to be any good to your students. Educators can be pretty selfless, but you do your students no favors if you are sick, sleep-deprived, angry at colleagues, anxious, depressed, or overwhelmed. There are many ways to do this, of course, and I've touched on some already. Taking care of yourself is a broad topic. It includes your physical, emotional, and social well-being—and I guess we could add spiritual, financial, and some other aspects!

I won't try to address the huge body of available tactics for self care. I just want to put this on your radar screen: You have to nourish yourself if you're to reach out to your students. They need trusting relationships with trustworthy, whole adults (at least as whole as possible). If the book had more chapters and more action steps, I'd suggest that you make an

In case of emergency, oxygen masks will drop from the ceiling.

Teachers please secure yours first before helping the students.

Whoa!

"oxygen-mask list." Set some goals for things you will do that are akin to putting the mask on yourself first.

Take Refuge

Are there days when you feel like you could barely face teaching your class? I'd be surprised if you did not answer "Yes." Everyone I know has these. No one escapes hardship; everyone experiences loss, pain, and disappointment. I know that all this talk about being an attractive, confident, caring educator can be maddening if your world is falling apart. There are times a teacher has to keep going in the face of adversity. (If you have yet to encounter significant life challenges, you must be pretty young!)

This book is not the place to address all the approaches, therapies, and ideas for holding things together at school when your world is falling apart. But, this book *is* about connection. So I want to plant this as a reminder and focus: True, trustworthy connections are the best things I know to help you do just that—hold together (or, for that matter, fall apart at the same time you keep some level of functioning). Nurture your relationships with friends, family, and colleagues so that they will be there for you in times of need. Be there for them, as well.

I'll insist until I am blue in the face that it is not your students' job to take care of your emotional needs or to be your support system. With that said, your job can become a refuge in troubling times. The joys of teaching, the fulfillment of helping students, and the satisfaction of those positive relationships you have built—all of those can be uplifting when your world becomes a nightmare.

Be aware that, even without disaster in your life, the relationships you build with students and colleagues at school feed you, too. Be open to the enrichment that a trusting student offers to your life.

You've Gotta Connect

Persist

I love one particular story about a woman who ran across the United States. I don't even know if the story is true. But the way it's told, her plan was to roughly follow the 40th parallel from the Jersey shore to San Francisco. She knew she was taking on a daunting task. So she decided that, instead of thinking about running across the whole country, she would just plan to run from one telephone pole to the next telephone pole.

She took her first stride. With smaller tasks instead of a monstrous project, the venture seemed less overwhelming. She found that running from pole to pole was all she had to think about. It was do-able! As she did this, her anxiety faded. After a time, she noticed and shouted, "Wow, I am already in Ohio!"

Looking for the next telephone pole.

Be like that woman. Don't compare yourself to the teachers that all the kids love. Don't think you have to run the race the way anyone else does it. Take one action step at a time; focus on getting from one kid to the next. Take note and before you know it, you may not be in Ohio, but you'll be well down the road to satisfying relationships with your students and all the benefits that come with those.

RESOURCES

Chapter 1
Resources and Research about Teacher-Student Relationships

Adler, N. (2002). Interpretations of the meaning of care: Creating caring relationships in urban middle school classrooms. *Urban Education, 37*(2), 241-266.

Anderman, L. H., & Freeman, T. M. (2004). Students' sense of belonging in school. In M. L. Maehr & P. R. Pintrich (Eds.), *Advances in motivation and achievement: Vol. 13. Motivating students, improving schools: The legacy of Carol Midgley* (pp. 27-63). Oxford: Elsevier JAI.

Bender, W. L. (2003). *Relational discipline: Strategies for in-your-face students*. Boston, MA: Pearson.

Bondy, E., & Ross, D. D. (2008). The positive classroom: The teacher as warm demander. *Educational Leadership, 66*(1), 54-58.

Bryk, A. S., & Schneider, B. (2002) *Trust in schools: A core resource for improvement*. New York, NY: Russell Sage Foundation.

Campbell, K., & Wahl, K. (2010). *A handbook for closing the achievement gap: SOAR*. Nashville, TN: Incentive Publications.

Campbell, K., & Wahl, K. (2012). *If you can't manage them, you can't teach them*. Nashville, TN: Incentive Publications.

Comer, J. P. (2004). *Leave no child behind*. New Haven, CT: Yale University Press.

Cornelius-White, J. (2007). Learner-centered teacher-student relationships are effective: A meta-analysis. *Review of Educational Research, 77*(1), 113-143.

Decker, D. M., Dona, D. P., & Christenson, S. L. (2007). Behaviorally at-risk African-American students: The importance of student-teacher relationships for student outcomes. *Journal of School Psychology, 45*(1), 83-109.

Furrer, C., & Skinner, E. A. (2003). Sense of relatedness as a factor in children's academic engagement and performance. *Journal of Educational Psychology, 95*(1), 148-162.

Hall, P. S., & Hall, N. D. (2003). Building relationships with challenging children. *Educational Leadership, 61*(1), 60-63.

Hymel, S., Schonert-Reichl, K. A., & Miller, L. D. (2006). Reading, 'riting, 'rithmetic and relationships: Considering the social side of education. *Exceptionality Education Canada, 16*(3), 149-192.

Konishi, C., Hymel, S., Zumbo, B. D., & Zehn, L. (2010). Do school bullying and student-teacher relations matter for academic achievement? *Canadian Journal of School Psychology, 25*(1), 19-39.

National Middle School Association (2010) *This we believe: Keys to educating young adolescents*. Westerville, OH: National Middle School Association.

Rogers, S., & Renard, L. (1999). Relationship-driven teaching. *Educational Leadership, 57*(1), 34-37.

Roorda, D. L., Koomen, H. M., Split, J. L., & Oort, F. J. (2011). The influence of affective teacher-student relationships on students' school engagement and achievement: A meta-analytic approach. *Review of Educational Research, 81*(4), 493-529

Schaps, E., Battistich, V., & Solomon, D. (2004). Community in school as key to student growth: Findings from the Child Development Project. In J. Zins, R. Weissberg, M. Wang, and H. Walberg (Eds.), *Building academic success on social and emotional learning: What does the research say?* (pp. 189-205). New York, NY: Teachers College Press.

Waters, J. T., Marzano, R. J., & McNulty, B. A. (2003). *Balanced leadership: What 30 years of research tells us about the effect of leadership on student achievement.* Aurora, CO: Mid-continent Research for Education and Learning.

Wentzel, K. (1997). Student motivation in middle school: The role of perceived pedagogical caring. *Journal of Educational Psychology, 89*(3), 411-419.

Wolk, S. (2003). Hearts and minds. *Educational Leadership, 61*(1), 14-18.

Wubbels, T. & Brekelmans, M. (2005). Two decades of research on teacher-student relationships in class. *International Journal of Educational Research, 43*(1-2), 6-24.

Zins, J. E., Bloodworth, M.R., Weissberg, R. P, & Walberg, H. (2004). The scientific base linking social and emotional learning to school success. In J. Zins, R. Weissberg, M. Wang, and H. Walberg (Eds.), *Building academic success on social and emotional learning: What does the research say?* (pp. 3-22). New York, NY: Teachers College Press.

Chapter 2

Kopkowski, C. (2008, April). Why they leave. *NEA Today*. Retrieved from www.nea.org/home/12630.htm.

Chapter 3

Klosterman, C. (October 23, 2007). Death by Harry Potter. *Esquire*. Retrieved from http://www.esquire.com/features/chuck-klostermans-america/klosterman1107.

Chapter 4

Pease, B., & Pease, A. (2006), *The definitive book of body language*. New York, NY: Bantam.

Strauss, N. (2005). *The game*. New York, NY: Harper Collins.

Chapter 6

Sarcasm definition. Retrieved from www.merriam-webster.com/dictionary/sarcasm.

Resources and Research about the Benefits and Effects of Humor

Adair, F. A., & Siegel, L. (1984). *Improving performance through the use of humor* (Report No. CG 017 783). New Orleans, LA: Southeastern Psychological Association. (ERIC Document Reproduction Service No. ED 250 584)

Caine, R. M., & Caine, G. (1991). *Making connections, teaching and the human brain*. Alexandria, VA: ASCD.

Caine, R. M., Caine, G., McClintic, C. L., & Klimek, K. J. (2004) *12 brain/mind learning principles in action: The fieldbook for making connections, teaching, and the human brain*. Thousand Oaks, CA: Corwin Press.

Chapman, A. J., & Foot, H. C. (Eds.). (1996). *Humor and laughter: Theory, research, and applications*. New Brunswick, NJ: Transaction.

Chapman, A. J., & Crompton, P. (1978). Humorous presentations of material and presentations of humorous material: A review of the humor and memory literature and two experimental studies. In M. M. Gruneberg, P. E. Morris, & R. N. Sykes (Eds.), *Practical aspects of memory* (pp. 84–92). London: Academic Press.

Edworthy, A. (2000). *Managing stress*. Buckingham, Great Britain: Open University Press.

Fine, G. A. (1983). Sociological approaches to the study of humor. In P. E. McGhee, & J. H. Goldstein (Eds.), *Handbook of humor research, volume I, basic issues* (pp. 159–181). New York, NY: Springer-Verlag.

Fry, W. F., & Salameh, W. A. (Eds.). (1987). *Handbook of humor and psychotherapy: Advances in the clinical use of humor*. Sarasota, FL: Professional Resource Exchange.

Goodman, J. (1983). How to get more smileage out of your life: Making sense of humor, then serving it. In P. E. McGhee, & J. H. Goldstein (Eds.), *Handbook of humor research, volume II, applied studies* (pp. 1–21). New York: Springer-Verlag.

Hobfoll, S. E. (1998). *Stress, culture, and community: The psychology and philosophy of stress*. New York: Plenum Press.

Hurren, B. L. (2010). *Humor in school is serious business*. Nashville, TN: Incentive Publications.

Hurren, B. L. (2006). The effects of principals' humor on teachers' job satisfaction. *Educational Studies, 32*(4), 373-385.

Lane, W. (1993). Strategies for incorporating humor into the school climate. *Schools in the Middle, 2*(4), 36-38.

Marlowe, J. (1995). The good, the bad, and the bozos. *Executive Educator, 17*(9), 24-26.

Martin, R. A. (2006). *The psychology of humor: An integrative approach*. Waltham, MA: Academic Press.

Martin, R. A. (2002) Is laughter the best medicine? *Current Directions in Psychological Science, 11*(6), 216-220.

Martin, R. A. (2001). Humor, laughter, and physical health: Methodological issues and research findings. *Psychological Bulletin, 127*(4), 504-519.

Moody, R. A. (1978). *Laugh after laugh*. Jacksonville, FL: Headwaters Press.

Pierson, P. R., & Bredeson, P. V. (1993). It's not just a laughing matter: School principals' use of humor in interpersonal communications with teachers. *Journal of School Leadership, 3*(5), 522-533.

Schmidt, S. R., & Williams, A. R. (2001). Effects of humor on sentence memory. *Journal of Experimental Psychology: Learning, Memory, and Cognition, 20*(4), 953–967.

Ziegler, V., Boardman, G., & Thomas, M. D. (1985). Humor, leadership, and school climate. *The Clearing House, 58*(8), 346–348.

Ziv, A. (1976). Facilitating effects of humor on creativity. *Journal of Educational Psychology, 68*(3), 318–322.

You've Gotta Connect